FINDING YOUR ELV

"You can only write a book like this if you have done a lot of soulful living. That means turning over a lot of stones, having some of them fall on your head—or your heart—and along the way finding some that are pure gold. As an author, Søren shares all that and more on his journey deep into the mysteries of the ElvenHeart. You'll know if you are called. We are in the midst of a renaissance, a returning to an awareness of ancient earthly wisdom, and Søren is on the forefront of this urgent remembering. As a courageous guide he is making a path we all can learn from. This book is both inspiring and practical— I was deeply moved."

— **CARL AUSTIN HYATT**, fine art photographer, shamanic workshop leader, and facilitator of corporate leadership retreats

"*Finding Your ElvenHeart* is truly visionary. It invites readers to connect not just with the Sidhe but with a future of true wholeness— both individual and collective. In the course of the book, Søren makes clear that the separation between humans and the Sidhe reflects a deeper separation from our own capacity for joy, for aliveness, and ultimately from aspects of our true selves. But the joy and wonder of this book is that working with the Sidhe becomes a path to the greater aliveness that we forgot."

— **THOMAS MILLER,** Co-creative Spirituality conference director, Findhorn Foundation

Finding Your
ELVEN
HEART

Working with the
Inner Realm of the Sidhe

Søren Hauge

FINDHORN PRESS

Findhorn Press
One Park Street
Rochester, Vermont 05767
www.findhornpress.com

Text stock is SFI certified

Findhorn Press is a division of Inner Traditions International

Disclaimer
The information in this book is given in good faith and intended for
information only. Neither author nor publisher can be held liable by
any person for any loss or damage whatsoever which may arise from
the use of this book or any of the information therein.

Cataloging-in-Publication data for this title
is available from the Library of Congress

ISBN 978-1-64411-149-9 (print)
ISBN 978-1-64411-150-5 (ebook)

Printed and bound in the United States by Lake Book Manufacturing, Inc.
The text stock is SFI certified. The Sustainable Forestry Initiative®
program promotes sustainable forest management.

10 9 8 7 6 5 4 3 2 1

Edited by Michael Hawkins
Text design and layout by Anna-Kristina Larsson
This book was typeset in Garamond and Cinzel

To send correspondence to the author of this book,
mail a first-class letter to the author c/o Inner Traditions •
Bear & Company, One Park Street, Rochester, VT 05767, USA
and we will forward the communication, or contact
the author directly at www.sorenhauge.com

Dedicated to The Sidhe

And to the Gentle Wildness
in you and me

CONTENTS

PART ONE
THE SIDHE

"For we who ride the winds,
run on the waves, and dance upon the mountains,
are more light than dewdrops on the banners of the dawn."

William Butler Yeats
The Land of Heart's Desire

"And all I thought of heaven before, I find in earth below:
A sunlight in the hidden core to dim the noonday glow."

George William Russell (AE)
A New World

FOREWORD

By David Spangler

I have had the pleasure of knowing Søren Hauge for many years and have enjoyed the privilege of calling him my friend. I have viewed him as an outstanding and innovative spiritual teacher. Yet, in spite of our friendship, our paths rarely crossed. His work was in Europe, mine in the United States; he was busy developing SoulFlow, and I was busy helping develop Incarnational Spirituality. We each had our spheres of operation and work, united in our desire to see a more harmonious world emerge but separated by distance and different responsibilities.

This was changed by the Sidhe. Whether these spiritual cousins of humanity set out to do so, I have no idea, but in unexpected ways, the Sidhe entered both of our lives and the result has been a delightful and mutually beneficial convergence of our work and our paths.

I knew of the Sidhe both from Celtic lore and from the pioneering work of my friend, John Matthews, whose book, *The Sidhe*, is a classic in this area and a beginning point for many of us. But I was not seeking to contact these beings and frankly, gave them little thought until one day, out of the blue, one of them appeared to me and said we had work to do together. The result was the *Card Deck of the Sidhe*, co-created with my Lorian colleague, Jeremy Berg.

This was a set of cards presented to us by the Sidhe as a tool people could use to contact them and form alliances of service on behalf of the earth.

At this point, the Sidhe became an important part of my life, and I was amazed and affirmed to discover that the same had been happening on the other side of the world to my friend, Søren. We were simultaneously having different yet complementary experiences with these beings. As a consequence, where our work had been different, we now found ourselves sharing a common project of helping the Sidhe make their presence known once more to modern society as they seek to help humanity at a time of planetary crisis and change.

This book arises out of this project, and I am honored to write this foreword.

ElvenHeart approaches the Sidhe from two important directions. On the one hand, it offers a deep look at the history and lore surrounding these beings. Drawing on his own rich experiences and on the insights and experiences of many others whose lives have intersected with the Sidhe, Søren helps us understand just who these beings are and why their presence is important to us and to our world.

The other gift this book offers is to encourage and guide us to finding the spirit of the Sidhe within ourselves. This is not just a mystical or metaphysical quest. The Sidhe call themselves our spiritual cousins and announce themselves as a branch of humanity that did not take the plunge into physical incarnation in the way we did. In effect, we are one species that split eons ago to occupy two different dimensions of the earth, each a complement to the other. We share a common spiritual ancestry, which means that just as the chemistry of the ancient seas out of which we physically emerged is present in our blood, so the qualities and magic of the Sidhe are present in us as well as part of our spiritual heritage. Awakening to this Sidhe-humanity within us in order to discover the joyful and rich—Søren would say, "wild"—wholeness of who we are is the second important theme of this book.

Søren addresses both these themes—the nature of the Sidhe and the nature of the Sidhe within us—with humor, compassion, and wisdom. He is forthright and down-to-earth, truly a practical mystic interested not in lofty spiritual ideals but in how we can help heal and bless our world through engagement with the Sidhe-half of our humanity. He is interested in actions, both inner and outer, and this book rings with the possibilities of what can be achieved as we open to our "ElvenHeart".

For this is the vitally important subtext of all Søren is doing and writing as a teacher and an emissary for the Sidhe: our earth is facing a moment of destiny when we will determine if we will continue as an evolving and thriving species or if we will lose all we have gained in the throes of a world turned practically uninhabitable as a result of selfish and short-sighted actions. We are faced with the choice of learning to be whole beings participating in the wholeness of a living and interconnected world or of continuing with our fragmentation and separation and seeing all our hopes for the future dashed.

The Sidhe are re-emerging in our time both to warn us and, most importantly, to partner with us in a reclamation of our ancient wholeness—a wholeness desperately needed if we are to be healers of the world and of ourselves. Many people around the world are being contacted and are heeding this message, opening to their own Elven-Hearts in their own way and thus being pioneers of hope.

Søren's book is an affirmation of this hope and a guide to finding our wild and creative wholeness. It is another step along the way to a deeper understanding of both the Sidhe and of ourselves, another step in bringing into being a new earth that is a blessing to all life.

David Spangler is a spiritual philosopher, educator, and writer. The co-founder and spiritual director of the Lorian Association, David is passionate about Incarnational Spirituality. His books include *Holding Wholeness in a Challenging World* and *Working with Subtle Energies*, and the *Card Deck of the Sidhe* (with Jeremy Berg). **www.lorian.org**

Introduction

Showing a new pathway can be a challenging task as you must confront the status quo and prepare yourself to be met with skepticism, and disputed with all kinds of questions. When I started teaching Theosophy in Denmark more than 35 years ago, I was met by strange questions by people full of doubts. Relatively basic topics like reincarnation, near-death-experiences, auras or meditation were met with many and often strange objections from people who were interested, and at the same time full of reservation. Today mainstream mentality has opened to many of these themes and mindfulness and holistic interests have become widespread in culture and society in many places around the world. Even the existence of angels, or whatever they are called around the globe, has become widely accepted across cultures and nations.

In many ways, writing about the Sidhe is a new frontier, and there is the risk of being ridiculed and seriously questioned. Even the name itself may be difficult to use, as it is not pronounced as it is written. The word *Sidhe* is Irish Gaelic and pronounced "she". There are quite a few books about the Sidhe already, and as a matter of fact, it is not even a new theme as they have been described for ages in different cultures. In Ireland, *Sidhe* is a well-known word. Nevertheless, this important topic, and what it implies, has not caught the attention of wider circles yet. I am convinced this will soon change and one day become mainstream knowledge like Mindfulness.

This Book Has a Dual Purpose

First, it answers the question: Who are the Sidhe? Why is it relevant and important that we learn about them, and how can we engage in a relationship with these beings? To me it is equivalent to asking a European why it should be relevant to know about an African or an Indonesian, and why we should connect with people from these areas. Add to the equation that there is a doubt if the Sidhe do exist at all, and why they are not just superstition or fiction, inventions of the subconscious or wishful thinking, and we are right at the crux of the task. My answer is, the Sidhe does not stop to exist simply because we doubt about them, and it is important that we are willing to be open to their existence.

Secondly, it takes the whole thing much further by stating that we Humans and the Sidhe have a shared past, and because of this we have something crucial in common. As we have come apart, we have developed differently, and each of us hold a clue to something important for the other. So, a possible encounter can become a beginning, not only for a kind of family union across borders, but also for an adventure of unlocking and unfolding our inner, forgotten nature. We humans hold a forgotten Sidhe-seed within us, and the Sidhe hold a neglected Human-seed within them.

If you can accept that this physical world or dimension is only a limited part of a grand scale of realms or dimensions in the larger reality, and that we all originate from a Divine source of all creation, you should be able to follow this book from start to end—and hopefully become inspired and ignited with something wonderful. The existence of subtle worlds is part of the greater ecology of Gaia or the Earth, and the Sidhe are part of it just like Angels and Nature

Spirits and other beings, including Humans that are not incarnated now. We are all part of the greater ecology—physically and more subtle.

This book unfolds what the Sidhe are and how we relate to them. At the same time, it invites you on a journey to start unfolding your inner Sidhe nature in order to become a more whole human being. It is a most wonderful adventure and exploration. It is ancient and yet very new. In my own personal life it has had a tremendous influence on how I approach each day, and in recent years it has affected my way of living, my attitude towards myself and others, how I work and how I look at life in ways great and small. As it has been transformative to myself, I have witnessed how it has created similar reactions in other people. Working with the Sidhe and with our own inner Sidhe nature has practical consequences.

I want to share the essence of this with you. The first part of this book, "*The Sidhe*", introduces the hidden people, and I share not only my own, but also other people's personal experiences of the Sidhe and their own inner Sidhe nature. From there the second part, "*The Wild Quest*", invites you on a personal journey to start unfolding your inner Sidhe nature—all the way to your ElvenHeart. In this part I share from my own life and how I have felt the influence of engaging with this multilayered and dynamic field. I am convinced that you can become deeply inspired and ignited, not only to a new way of action and engagement with the world around you, but also to a new approach to your very being and essence. Even though there will be many things that are related to numerous contemporary approaches to spirituality, I am certain that there is real and reliable innovation at hand in all that this approach implies and leads to—and I am excited to share it with you. So, let's engage!

Søren Hauge
Kisserup, Lejre, Denmark 2020

THE SIDHE

Something wonderful awaits us.
It is in the outskirts of our memory,
And closer to us than we ever thought.
A family reunion is at hand.
It is highly disturbing to the status quo,
Yet, dear to our very core.
You are invited!

I

THE HIDDEN PEOPLE

◯ *A Conversation between Two Sidhe* ◠

Two Sidhe sit together in their world, having a conversation about the wonders of life. Their speech is more like a song than speech, but they communicate in their ordinary way while they exchange matters of interest in their own humming style. One of the Sidhe is a tall, slender and graceful male with pointed ears and wild hair, almost like a fan around his head. He is very young and eager, and he is disturbed by the fact that lately his world has been shaken—it clearly has disturbed him. The other Sidhe obviously belongs to the Elders amongst them. He has lived for a long time and experienced earlier times and many places full of wonder. Now they sit together at a flowing river, surrounded by rainbow-colored birds dancing in the light from the bright green fields of grass.

"Do you believe in humans?", the young and excited Sidhe asks with a slightly strained look that does not seem to be his natural disposition. He is worried for that which has interrupted his world and the question is very much on his mind. He emanates great skepticism, but he also seems to be slightly haunted by the question.

The old Sidhe looks at the young one with a scrutinizing glance engaged in the past, the present and the future at the same time. With a deep, peaceful voice his singing returns to the young Sidhe: *"We are called the Sidhe and not without reason. We are dancers in the gentle, wild wind, and it is our nature not to become too fixed and rigorous.*

Therefore, be open my young friend of the wind. Yes, humans do exist. You often sense them as dark shadows passing by or as dense, rigid spheres. They are somewhat at our size, but they do look very heavy and dense."

The young Sidhe looks with disbelief at the Elder: *"You can't be serious? The gloomy shadows you describe are lifeless echoes from something long gone. What should our business be with them? I have a hard time believing that you really mean this."*

The old Sidhe smiles whimsically: *"You have kept these dark orbs too much at a distance—and you know it is not our nature to distance anything. Try to take a look with me right now. There is a group of them right there."*

The young Sidhe stares, slightly scared and with some disgust at the solid lumps that move along at the edge of the Sidhe realm like some kind of zombies or spooky echoes. Nevertheless, he chose to continue observing them, unlike what he normally does. Time goes and he doesn't think anything happens. His facial expression shifts between determination, slight discomfort and a flickering change as he attempts to overcome his tendency to resist. *"They seem almost lifeless and they emanate a rather monotone noise."*

"Yes," the old Sidhe answers, *"but look deeper, connect with the presence behind the shell, almost as if you look into a dense thicket."*

The young Sidhe continues to stare, almost as if it is a riddle he must solve, or a trick needing to be revealed. His eyes quiver and he remains perplexed as he senses the loud noise surrounding the tedious, disturbing lumps. Never has he looked so much at the dried, dark tubers, and he is on the brink of giving up when he suddenly detects that inside the heavy, messy wilderness there is something. First, he senses it as a weak clearing that comes and goes, but finally he gets a glimpse of a flickering light far, far inside the murky thicket. He is struck by surprise and his eyes light up in confusion and disbelief. *"You are right. There is something in there! What on Earth is it?!"*

The old Sidhe breaks out in a big, warm smile: *"It is the flame of hope and it is very special as it grows when you stay with it. The flame is a light from the forgotten human heart, and NOW you know why we are a bunch amongst us who have initiated a completely new journey into unknown territory. We simply KNOW that here something is hiding and waiting to be met. Humans do exist and they are our ancient relatives. You probably know the ancient legends about our forgotten Hallows and the magic that disappeared from the world above us, and our touch of melancholy. Humans are NOT just myth and humbug. They exist and they live—but their light is imprisoned in the thicket of cynicism and the darkness of isolation."*

The young Sidhe looks with big eyes of disbelief at the old one: *"So what then? Are WE really going to save them? Are you serious? Would it not be better to leave them on their own so they can find their way and wake up? I mean, they can't handle us!"*

The old one waits for a while and when silence has become penetrating, he continues in a quiet tone: *"Some of the wise amongst us who have been here for a long time, have discovered that we actually need something from our human relatives, just like they can benefit from contact with us. We originate from the same root and the myths about our separation are not just fiction. It is a great and wondrous journey towards a new future where we can find each other again in some way or another. My dear young friend, the thing is that many like you doubt that the humans exist. So, why should any good things come out of a journey towards an unknown place? They believe that such a thing would be futile. You have just discovered the flame of hope in the seemingly lifeless humans, and you can actually embark on this journey if you want. We need young blood. We call the adventure towards the new future 'The Journey to The Forgotten Land'. Think about it and if you want to participate, let me know. You are welcome. I mean, come with us, if you cannot resist it. The traveling company towards The Forgotten Land bids you welcome if you are ready for the adventure. Humans are real—they live—and we have very valuable things to discover and to share with each other. The future has a new possible course and it seems the timing is now more than ever before."*

At the Outer Headland

I lead a Sidhe-workshop in the city of Aarhus in Denmark and as there is an uneven number of participants during exercises, I have stepped in as partner for one of the participants. We make a guided imaginary journey to our Sidhe-relatives and see what may emerge. During the part where I am being guided by the other person it comes to me with some surprise that I am going to an important place. After the initial anchoring and honoring life around me, I open myself to the inner journey. Suddenly there is a shift within me. I fly over huge landscapes in the North and sense the atmosphere of pine forests passing beneath me. It is somewhat surprising as I mostly expected to facilitate the participant I am partnered with for the exercise, and not to engage deeply myself. Now I open my inner life to the great, Nordic landscapes as I sense how I am traveling far away to places where humans rarely appear—if at all.

The atmosphere of great sceneries and majestic forests becomes more massive and after a while I sense that I am losing height, descending in order to land. Ahead of me I see a rocky headland at the outer edge of a seemingly endless coniferous forest. I sense the atmosphere of the sea and I am naturally drawn to the place. I feel deeply connected with it. Pine trees have always had a special meaning to me, a sense of being at home, and meeting such trees at the sea strikes me and sets a note of lyrical upliftment, opening up to the beauty and wonder of life, right there at the edge between land and sea.

Then I see him, sitting there on the outer rock. He is turned towards the sea, so I see him from the back. His figure is full of calmness. He is clad in a form of cape or mantle, looking like his dress and at the same time to be extended into the landscape as if he is clad in nature, wrapped in the essence of rocks and pine trees. He has dark hair and it seems as if he has some kind of headdress—or it may be his hair, I am not sure. However, one thing is certain, he is singing, singing to the sea, to the sky, to the rocks and to the forest. Or no, he is not singing to them, he is singing with them. The song is magnificent and diversified, almost as an entire orchestra in itself—and yet very simple in a way I can't explain. It is as if he is weaving or braiding connections, both strengthening and renewing already existing ones and creating new ones, vibrating them into the already existing web. In some way I sense that he is weaving an extract of his human contact into the living threads of song-lines he is upholding and creating. I sense a multicolored aura around him, very delicate like a scent, and in a marvelous way he is in the forest, at the sea, in the air and down in the massive rocks as he is weaving and singing there on the headland where land and water meet.

While he is singing and the tunes emanate their rich colors, I also pick up that time is so different to him than to my consciousness. He has a part of him way back in days gone by, but for him they are not gone at all. At the same time, he reaches out into the not yet manifested future, while he is deeply anchored in the living present. It is as if he is singing the past, present and future together, and in the midst of it I suddenly see pictures of a smaller village in his world. It is somewhat like an outpost to more populated areas in his Sidhe-realm. The village is far out in the big forests and yet in a transition to more populated areas. He is in a world bordering to mine and where he is now, he feels most at home, but from time to time he is also in his village or hamlet where he is together with others. I sense that he is in a greater transition himself and in contacting me he has revitalized an old connection and renewed his commitment to reach out to humans—I being one of them. Old and new meet—a different pathway has opened and after a long time he has said yes to this.

Now he is sitting there at the outer headland, singing, and his song carries new tunes. He is a WindSinger, weaving new life through the treads of the song-lines, and I sense that the new facets are connected to the fact that my human world in some way has been invited into the song as he has decided to contact humanity again. I say again as way back in his time there was contact, and somewhere in the tapestry I am part of that greater pattern being weaved with many others.

Scarcely I register that in a moment the window to his world will be closing, but also that my glimpse into it is part of the opening I have dedicated myself to. Soon after I open my eyes and share some of it with my partner, feeling a great warmth within me. The journey of the WindSinger is on the move and this is a moment in the great, flowing timeline, sweeping forward towards The Forgotten Land and its discovery.

Fjeldur

Since the fragile beginning in 2012 I have had many encounters with my Sidhe-friend. Supported by my friend and colleague, David Spangler, I started trusting my impressions and gradually began to understand the nature of my contact. It took courage and determination to stay on track. My background in Theosophy had made it easy for me to embrace the existence of angels, devas and nature spirits, but to me the Sidhe was—in a way—something completely new. I had not come across them, or if I had, I am sure I would interpret them as belonging to the devic, angelic or nature spirit realm. Now I realized that this was not the case at all. To use an unprecise analogy it is like seeing people at a distance, just calling them people, while they are actually quite different in culture, language and habits when perceived at a closer range, belonging to different continents, nations and religions, with a great variety of folklore, different history and customs. So, humans are not just humans. Likewise, non-human beings can be categorized in very broad terms while they are incredibly diverse.

The discovery of the existence of the Sidhe was a great relief to me. It felt like important pieces to a grand puzzle fell into place. Starting to understand the nature of their being, I also realized how it could be possible to label them as devic-angelic or as forms of nature spirits. This is what I had been doing previously. Later in this book I will share much more about the nature of the Sidhe, compared to other beings. For now, I just want to expand a little about the nature of my Sidhe contact. In 2012 David Spangler conducted an online seminar about the Sidhe. It was his first of this kind, and to me it was a completely new door opening, and yet an opportunity to discover that I felt a deep recognition from the core of my being. Together with his colleague Jeremy Berg, he also introduced The Sidhe Card Deck as a new tool to connect with the Sidhe and especially the Sidhe nature in ourselves. The seminar was a revelation to me, and it ignited something of immense significance within me. It started a chain reaction: Within me something was afoot, and on the outer front I knew I would end up making workshops about the theme.

Jeremy's artistic attunement to the Sidhe via the cards was deeply inspiring, and David's sharings from the female Sidhe he communicated with was crammed with openings, insights and new dimensions I had to take in and assimilate it all in my life. Intentionally the female Sidhe, who David called Mariel, wanted the cards to be gateways to our own inner Sidhe nature, and not portraits of Sidhe that could create a hype around exotic beings and create a serious blockage for a renewed contact between the Sidhe and humanity. It was clear that the romantic, devotional approach to the Sidhe was exactly what was *not* wanted as it would make the intended partnership almost impossible. Mariel emphasized that the Sidhe who invited this new connection wished to create a possible cooperation between equals, and not a repetition of the old approach. The Sidhe was to be considered as co-travelers on the path of awakening, and a renewed connection between them and us was an opportunity that could bring hope and new friendships.

To me this was spiritual sanity at its best, and I resonated deeply with the mentality Mariel emphasized. At the same time, it touched something deeply within myself as I was sensing some kind of inner movement. In the beginning it came across in a recognition of the Sidhe realm. I sensed it as a reality in the same way as I sense how it is to experience the atmosphere of a city. A part of me was picking up an atmosphere from the Sidhe world—a mixture of intense nature, saturated with a presence resembling we humans, and with a touch of melancholy. So, for weeks I had the feeling that a part of me was present in two realms simultaneously. One was in my own world, and another was in a world where the green connectedness of nature was mingled with beings closely related to us, yet slightly removed. They were not humans and not angels or nature spirits, but somewhere in between, yet closest to we humans.

In the center of all this, something was happening, and step by step I realized that a specific being from this realm was approaching me. During several months I had new experiences that needed much adjustment and acceptance from myself. Strangely enough, my Theosophical background was both a help and a hindrance. I was "raised" to believe that real "messengers" to humanity only contacted rare, selected disciples of highly trained capacity, such as Geoffrey Hodson, Alice Ann Bailey or other global trailblazers. The very thought that "someone" reached out to me who was simply a dedicated Dane, created doubts and challenges. I had to overcome this resistance and realize that it was *a must*—I simply had to accept the invitation. I would betray my innermost if I stepped back. After all, it was not a spiritual guide that wanted to channel messages through me. Rather, it was as if it was an old friend who reached out and invited me into a partnership of mutual inspiration.

Gradually, and with encouragement from David, I found it easier to deal with, and the inner contact from the male Sidhe evolved. It happened during several occasions in 2012 and 2013. What I was realizing was that a likeminded individual from the Sidhe realm invited me to a continued cooperation that could be of mutual benefit. We had a shared interest in language or expression—he as a singer in his world, and I as a teacher, coach and author in my world. I also realized that he had a deep interest in what I would call the Nordic world and what it could mean to help this area of the planet to awaken in new ways. Finally, but not the least, he also had a keen interest in how we can help the planet, Gaia, to be appreciated in new ways, and how we can enhance this by activating new dimensions within ourselves and let it inspire new actions in our respective worlds. This was the powerful incentive for me to start facilitating Sidhe workshops and writing books about the Sidhe.

How did the contact evolve? Well, many pieces make the puzzle, but at an early stage I felt his presence as a breath from a pine forest and a need to sit down and meditate. When doing so I sensed him as an erect, male presence who intended to share important things with me. I leaned in and felt a merging between him and me, and the condensed atmosphere was permeated with pine trees, wind and open space. I sensed how his intentions could emerge in my mind in a way so I could transform it into words, and so I wrote down, to the best of my abilities, what was on his mind. At the end of the first intention I wrote down, I suddenly added "Fjeldur" and "Fjelduria" in a bracket. Immediately I dismissed it and found it again several months later when I looked at the words I wrote. Reading the name again I realized I had to take it seriously—so in my world his name is Fjeldur, but the inner meaning of it is *a mountain full of music."* When I shared this with David at an early stage, he replied that he sensed Fjeldur so clearly in exactly that description.

Fjeldur is a word resembling words from Iceland and the Faroe Islands, but I did not have a clue about it when I wrote it. If I should try to use it as a gateway to him, I would say that it is a Nordic name and he probably has a special connection to the Faroe Islands although I sense him close to me when there is contact. He is occupied in this own world, as I have tried to share a tiny bit of, earlier in this book, but when I sense him, it is mostly a recognition of vibration or identity, similar to how I recognize the distinct atmosphere of my brother or my daughters or someone I know. In the early stages there were visual impressions and smells, especially of moss, heather and fir trees. This can be the case today as well, but if I can explain it very simply, it is as if I lean my heart and mind into his, and in the shared space of our heart-minds there is an exchange of impressions and intentions.

How is he as an identity? He is a mixture of old traditions and very unconventional improvisation. He is like a deeply rooted mountain or a landscape, pervaded by a living wind full of sounds. He is ancient, yet curious like a young man, and he has humor. He is a sound-lover and a sound-creator. He is a noble presence, erect and stately—yet full of flowing, whirling playfulness. As a kind of paradox, he relies on ancient insight and questions any blind authorities. He never seems to be afraid of doing things in new ways that break convention. In his world he is part of a fellowship and a local settlement as well. I don't have many details about this, but it is important to him. He is a landscape guardian, a representative of "Nordica"—a phrase David coined during one of our talks about Fjeldur—and deeply committed to the family reunion of Humanity and the Sidhe. He is learning about Humanity through me, and surely also through many others he may sense, and his intensity is released in potent packages of interest that end up in my mind as words and sentences. So, any words from him are mine. They are my responsibility. I do my best to paint on his canvas when I share his intentions.

Fjeldur is not a human being. He is a Sidhe and he does not perceive my world with human psychology but through his nature which is something different. When I ask him to give a perspective on the inner nature of the wind, because I feel that the wind in my life has overturned me and affected my balance, he does not engage deeply with my human challenges, but shares a perspective from his world:

"We are the People of the Wind, but we have many names in your world, also beyond the areas of the world you have investigated until now. Very often we are connected with the wind, the air, the storms, for we are dancers in the wind and sing its songs. I am glad to share a view on the wind for your inspiration.

"Everything breathes. Do you notice this? Everything breathes as it is part of the wind of life, the breath of the spirit. Even that which seems to be most quiet is breathing. Perhaps you do not notice it, but in some way, it is breathing. We the Sidhe easily pick up this movement as something natural, inner and outer, everywhere and at any time.

"You are also a being of the wind. May I remind you that you carry the wind in yourself. Think of your breath. For you it might feel as if you mostly breathe at a certain place in your body. Still, you might also sense that you can experience your breath and a waving rhythm, spreading out into your whole body. This is something you know from traditions you have where the breath is used to create calmness and connect with flow. For us the breath is something that sweeps through our entire form, and it does not stop there. We do not experience a limit like you do—so the breath is also around us. We do not primarily breathe inside our bodies; we breathe in and with the world we are part of in our natural connectedness. The breath is drawn through us, more than we mainly breathe ourselves. It is different to us than to you. We always sense we are in a greater breath and this cyclic pulse is the wind we are always part of. We are within the wind and it blows through us. Because of this we are not 'hit' by the wind from outside, but it is much more the pulse that is expressed in us. We live in the wind. We breathe and we are being breathed—and we are perpetually in this huge pulse.

"Perhaps it is easier if you think of fish in the sea. They let the water come through their gills as they flow through the liquid element of water, continually affected by waves and streams. In this way we are always in the huge, living sea of air. We are not overturned as easily as you are, and I mean it literally and metaphorically. You cannot simply be like me because we are different. I am more unified with the wind and in a way, I become the form or face of the wind. You are denser and the wind hits you harder, but you can help yourself make a new covenant with the wind by experiencing how the breath is in your entire body, psyche and mind. This will help you experience that you are always in a windy landscape and you can learn to navigate the winds of life by attuning to the wind—the atmosphere and its conditions—where you are right now. We must become WindDancers. If we do not dance with the wind, it will dance us into pieces. It is a noble art to learn, a great adventure to embark on. In your life you are being tested by the winds of life. As the art is learnt you will begin breathing with the present, in you and around you. You become a WindNavigator and the nature of the wind becomes a part of you. In this sense you are not easily blown away."

Fjeldur knows that all speech comes from song. Originally, we are all singers and in a way speech and words can be seen as ice cubes and singing is like liquid water. It is the same element but in different conditions. We humans communicate mostly in "ice cube language" while the Sidhe prefer to communicate in "liquid language." We can understand each other with careful attention, but the fixed and chunky world of ice cubes is very different from the world of flowing waters and it is easy to misunderstand each other. Fjeldur has shared with me, that to him and his kin all song is a celebration of life and we are invited to partake in the great celebration. In doing so we can sing forth The Forgotten Land and begin experiencing that we are truly landing in the land of Gaia. This only becomes possible when we leave the mindset of separation and fixed matter. To follow his intention:

"We can invite you to the dance as we know the nature of dancing and have learnt the art of movement. It has taken us ages. It is our nature to weave bright connections and follow the flow of the moment, uniting and connecting. We braid and link. We merge threads and blow waves of living energy and we invite you to explore the unknown hiding in the twilight zone. We can shapeshift and float in the waters of the present while we listen to the music and tunes in everything. We can invite you to the song of the sirens and to the forbidden fruits because we know the hidden treasures behind the borders of routines. We make the ugly and the pretty converge in beauty where the wonder of life unfolds. We rejoice in the present and explore the nuances and facets of the moment with the energy that dances perpetually and sense wholeness in movement. We feel the song with our whole being, the song that bursts in all living processes and opens to the deep magic. We are wedded to connectedness, expanding and collecting in ever returning rhythms of ebb and flow. We follow the deep keynotes from the Earth below and stretch ourselves in the grand being above. The crystal-clear light from our hearts reflects the sparkling stars and play in the poetry of dewdrops. We are the green partners of Earth and the living artists of the fertile imagination—and we invite you to song, music and dance, from the resounding depth of mountains to the subtle notes of flower scents. This is our nature, our inheritance and our journey, and we invite you to new partnership, so we can find and enter The Forgotten Land."

It is easy to be overwhelmed by the realm of the Sidhe and not difficult to understand why the lore of the Sidhe is also tainted by warnings and admonitions. We can easily become enchanted by the lightness, the lyrical atmosphere and the sense of relief when encountering the fragrance of "Fairy Land." However, we must remember that our Sidhe relatives are not semi-gods and they evolve just like we, but in different ways. What could they possibly learn from us, one might ask? Well, to mention a few things, we have developed a stamina and standing power in the dense physicality that they find mysterious and full of riddles. We might be heavy and rigid, but we actually create in dense matter under hard conditions. They can learn from this. Because of our situation we are also learning a lot from separation, sorrow and loss, and the warm nature of our compassionate hearts has a different quality than the crystalline brightness of their hearts. They are drawn to the warmth and the glow of our nature. Because of this and other aspects we must not forget that *fellowship* and not "*follow-ship*" is the keynote of our mutual exploration when we decide to connect. We are possible partners—and I will get back to this important perspective later.

A Planetary Presence

From the early beginning since Fjeldur contacted me, he has given me a clear impression that his kin are everywhere on the globe, in their own realm, and he is only a Nordic representative of a species with many differing expressions, just like a person from the North European sphere is not able to represent all human cultures. His intention is clear: *"We are the forgotten people and yet we are remembered all over the world. See how many places you can find us, and you will be surprised, happily surprised."* This intention I have sensed from him many times, and I have followed his suggestion. I am already aware that Fjeldur and his kin are known as the Sidhe in the Celtic tradition and I will return to this. I am also very aware that the Sidhe are the same as what we know in the Nordic tradition under the names *Elves* and *Huldra* people. This goes for Scandinavia— Denmark and especially Norway and Sweden—but it also includes the Faroe Islands and not least Iceland.

Actually, in Iceland the *Huldufólk*, as they are called, are so well known in present time that there is a public awareness of them, even to such a degree that urban development and building of new roads take into consideration not to interfere with areas where Huldra people are supposed to be present in greater concentration. This is a unique situation, considering that Iceland has a population with advanced high tech and IT. It seems to be possible to mix a hyper-modern society with an ancient nature awareness. To a slightly lesser degree the Faroe Islands have an awareness of the Huldra people. On one of my trips to these unique islands the bus driver taking us from the airport told us spontaneously that certain rocks we passed were not removed *"as Huldra people live in them."* It could partly be a joke, but the very fact that he said it, shows something about the collective awareness on the Faroe Islands. In Norway, Sweden and especially Denmark it has more faded from collective memory, except if you ask historians, archeologists and people interested in Nordic folklore and mythology.

The word *Huldra* comes from the Nordic word "*hylle*" (tilhyllet), meaning hidden, covered or veiled, so the Huldra people are the secret or hidden people. When shown in the Nordic countries the Huldra people appear to look like us, but sometimes a partly hidden tale reveals that they are not ordinary people. Recent excavations made by archeologists in Denmark actually suggests that in the Middle Ages the Christian faith was mixed with a belief in the Huldra people as prayers to Christ has been found in folded lead-capsules, combining him with Huldra people. In Nordic mythology the *Huld* was also seen as the völva or seiðkona, a Nordic shaman who practiced seiðr (sejd), a magical approach to connect inner and outer reality, especially associated with the Goddess Freyja, the female dísir, and the God Odin. The Huld or Hulda could be seen as a human being relating to the Huldra through the practice of seiðr, the Nordic shamanic practice.

Another variation of traditions linking to the Sidhe are the different stories about selkies and mermaids, described in different but related ways in the Nordic and Northern European areas. The tales are about shapeshifting and about humans who get spellbound by the beauty of the Selkies. Sometimes they end up getting married and in certain stories it has severe consequences as the humans capture the selkies against their will. There is a recognizable atmosphere of melancholy and also fear and admonition surrounding these haunting stories.

When looking further beyond it is possible to discover much more. Further up North the Samish people have a tradition regarding the underworld people living in the mountains and the untouched nature. They are called *Ulda* (related to huldra) or *Gadniha*, and in southern Samish they are called *Saajve*. They look like humans and in their world, bordering ours, there is great happiness and wealth. They are known to live within the hills.

Down South in Europe the Romanians call this hidden people *Iele*, "beings" most often appearing as stunningly beautiful women that can have a seductive power over men from our human world— an image that is also seen in many other places, for instance amongst the Huldra women. They are also called *Zâne*, beings who resemble the famous *Graces* and who mostly live in the deep forests. They can be shapeshifters and according to tradition they can help humans traveling in nature, giving them symbols and signs to help them reach their destination. The word Zâne is connected with beauty. The Zâne are said to gift human children so they become good at dancing, develop beauty and kindness. There is also another variety called *Blajini*, who live in a kind of parallel world to ours. The word Blajini means kindhearted and these creatures are connected to the inner Earth. According to legend the Blajini and humans once lived together and the biblical story about Moses dividing the Sea symbolically marks the division between them and us.

In Bulgaria the same beings are called *Samodiva* and *Samovila*. The words are connected to divinity, remoteness and wildness. Again, the most prevalent descriptions portray the etheric, female Samodivas with long hair and sometimes even wings, clad in white garments. They are said to reside in dark caves, inside trees and in the Bulgarian mountains. They are known to be able to seduce human men because of their beauty. More than anything else they are known to dance, expressing the pure nature forces, especially the wind, and often accompanied by song.

Going all the way down to the Southern Hemisphere there is clear evidence of traditions regarding the hidden people and the legends, and myths have survived in the collective memory, including people who experience them today. Amongst the Australian Aboriginals there are descriptions of *Irrernte-arenye*, the spirits of the ancestors, guiding and protecting special sacred places while they sing in dreamtime. Illustrations of them by artists show gracious bodies in flowing, dancing postures, typical features of the Sidhe. In the neighboring country, New Zealand, the Maoris have the tradition about *Patupaiarehe*, sometimes called *Tūrehu* or *Pakepakehā*, perceived as pale or light, spiritual beings living in the depth of the forests and mountains of New Zealand and often sensed by humans with a peculiar, etheric flute-music and song. They are said to be able to lure humans away from safe surroundings with music and song and they possess magical skills and certain insights. Their skin normally is light and their hair reddish or light, and they are often experienced in twilight or when it is foggy. They have relatives called *Ponaturi*, unusual sea-creatures that only go on land during night and who resemble selkies from the Nordic tradition.

If we take the journey to the American continent, the Cherokee Indians have the living tradition about *Nûñnë̈ʾhï* (*Nunnehi*), *"the people who live anywhere,"* and who have been encountered vividly around and under the mountains and in the water. They are said to be a very benign people who are fond of music and dance. The example from the Cherokee is a sign of similar beliefs and traditions among all American Indian tribes.

These are examples of the many different names from numerous traditions around the globe where the shapeshifting beings dance and sing and hold the keys to a long, lost magic. The Greek *Nymphs* and the Slavic *Vilas*, who rule over the wind and live in hills and mountains, are other examples of openings to the remote and yet present world of the Sidhe. I am certain that the list will become much, much longer if an extensive investigation into myths and traditions regarding the Sidhe is made from all corners of the world.

Through all the variations there are several recurring features, describing an almost invisible people, partly spiritual, partly earthly, living in nature or behind nature, intimately connected with mountains, forests and water, especially far out in the wilderness. They are deeply associated with all sentient beings. They are not always friendly towards humans, but it clearly seems to relate to a lack of understanding and respect that has created misunderstandings and separating walls, like our tensions between human cultures and religions.

It is obvious that the stories about hauntingly beautiful creatures that seduce humans—often men—with their graceful and sensual looks, music and song, is a frequent element, just like the fact that we humans can benefit from contacts with them if we respect them properly. There is fear-based superstition in most of the traditions, as well as contradictory statements pointing at an ambivalence towards the hidden people. In Christianity, they have been demonized as fallen angels, and therefore extremely dangerous as they could tempt humans and bring them to perdition and damnation. The luring and seducing aspects, especially the female expressions, like the Greek *Sirens*, are so clearly related to divided and conflicting relations to sexuality, sensuality, nature, women and the beauty of the body, so frequently shown in the history of Christianity in our part of the world.

The Riders of the Sidhe—John Duncan, 1911
The Sidhe as a dignified people in procession—
carrying the Four Hallows

Behind the myths and legends there is a living reality, colored by our cultural, religious and social traditions and mentality. Delving into at least some of the variations has provided me with so many details about a global phenomenon, and I am convinced that time will open a new window for our growing recognition of these relatives, seeing them once again as real, existing beings and not just products of human inventiveness. As so often, creative imagination draws on something from the existing reality. From Tolkien's *Elves* to the movie *Avatar* with the blue *Na'vi* ("The People") and further into the multiple online games where Elves play an important part of the many roles the gamers can play.

We modern humans tend to distance ourselves from approaches to reality that does not seem to fit into the technological paradigm of computers and scientific language. We tend to smile at perspectives not encompassed by calculating rationality, entirely forgetting that the evidence-based intellect is only a small part of the totality we call reality. There is so much beyond the borders of prevalent logic and the dominant, materialistic life-view. When we dare leave the comfort-zone of industrial efficiency, we might discover that something incredibly surprising awaits us. This extended reality does not cancel conventional science—on the contrary it is a gift, only expanding our bandwidth of accepted reality. The Sidhe awaits us just across the border, and they are so much more than folklore and fear-based folk tales that too often are religiously interpreted and characterized by ignorance and superstition.

The Irish Connection

Ireland is one of the places in the world where the knowledge and experiences of the Sidhe is most extensive. After all, Sidhe is also the Irish-Gaelic word I have chosen to use as the primary name for our closest Gaian relatives. Although superstition and fear-tainted aspects also color the Irish tradition to some extent, it is so much alive even today, and full of detail, that it is worth staying with it for a while. In the Irish tradition there has been a strong and powerful line of Sidhe-awareness for ages, and the Irish history has the Sidhe interwoven as an important part of the development of the country and its identity.

According to legend the Sidhe were a people, *Tuatha Dé Danann*, who came from the West to Ireland and settled on the green isle. They brought with them skills in art, crafting and magic, so the saying goes, and they became the ruling tribe in Ireland until another arriving group from the South, the Milesians, challenged them. After a battle they agreed to divide Ireland. It was decided that the

Milesians would live above the ground, and they became the Gaelic people of Eire. Tuatha Dé Danann would inhabit Ireland beneath the ground and they became the Sidhe, living in the Underworld or the Otherworld. In this way—so is the story—the division between "us" and "them" became a fact, and through this mythical-historical tale Tuatha Dé Danann are placed in a form of parallel world or realm situated under or behind our physical world. Sometimes this realm is called Tír na nÓg, the land of eternal youth. This population in the world beneath our world has been called by many names: *Aos Sí, The Sidhe, the People of the Mounds, The Good Neighbors, The People of Peace, The Good People, The Gents* or simply *The People,* just to mention some. Confusingly enough they have also been called *The Faery People* or The *Fay*—making many people mistake them for being some kind of nature spirits like flower fairies or other beings solely connected with trees, rivers, rocks or other aspects with nature.

According to David Spangler's female Sidhe-contact, the story about Humanity and the Sidhe is a tale about one huge flood of living beings, originally one species in its root, gradually dividing in the ancient past, way back before recorded history, and finally becoming like two separated deltas of species in the great flow of evolution. This was before we even manifested in the physical world. One part of the river of beings started to descend vertically into dense matter, ending up as we human beings, but another part of the huge stream diverted and developed an interest in descending in a sloping way. These beings did not manifest in the dense, centered way like us, but went more into what we might call the peripheral part of the planes of manifestation. They are known today as the Sidhe. Just as Humanity is full of diversity and differing characteristics, the Sidhe are extremely diverse and this description is therefore a broad generalization. However, it is not misleading to say that we are more dense and solid than the Sidhe, and yet they are also incarnated on wavelengths that can be called physical. Normally we cannot sense them, but there are numerous stories about meetings between Humans and Sidhe—in fact there is a rich lore about it in many cultures and traditions.

We humans are very solid and live in the heavier parts of the manifested worlds, while our Sidhe relatives are more energetical with a plasticity foreign to us. To us the Sidhe are in the outskirts of the manifested worlds. Because of this they live "behind," "under" or "beside" our realm, not being as compact and characterized by inertia than we are accustomed to. Sidhe and humans are branches on the same tree, and we have a shared root and shared potentials. Our starry nature is alike. This means that the Sidhe have seeds to evolve that we humans have unfolded, while we have seeds the Sidhe have unfolded. We share a common inheritance, but we have unfolded our spiritual DNA in different directions.

This implies that at a deeper level we can benefit greatly in connecting as we are each other's closest relatives. In the past there have been numerous confrontations between the Sidhe and Humanity, mainly because of misunderstandings and a lack of mutual respect. Because of this there is not a unanimous willingness on the side of the Sidhe to engage with us but increasing numbers of them attempt to build bridges. At a deeper level the reason is obvious. We need each other as inhabitants on the same planet and the present global crisis with all its different aspects affect the Sidhe in ways so they cannot ignore us. So, the call to reconnect and exchange in evolving understanding and friendly relations is very needed for Earth, or Gaia, as a whole. It is like a healing process or a possible family reunion.

However, there is another crucial part of the story, concerning you and me, and it is the fact that just as the Sidhe have within them seeds of Humanity, we have within us seeds of the Sidhe, which we can call our inner Sidhe-nature, or our Elvenforce, or whatever we choose to call this neglected treasure within us. Connecting with the Sidhe inevitably will stimulate this part of us, just as they are stimulated by us, and something within is accelerating in its unfoldment. So, you and I have within us undiscovered, or almost neglected aspects of our nature that can be found and opened. This is essential for us and therefore you are sitting with this book now. Later we will dedicate all our energy and attention to this very important endeavor and adventure.

William Butler Yeats   **George William Russell (AE)**

I find it important to include two Irish people at this stage. They were friends and they are both considered to be cultural pioneers in the recent Irish history. The most famous of them was William Butler Yeats (1865-1939), a huge figure in the Celtic Renaissance of Ireland and a literary giant in the 20th century, awarded the Nobel Prize in Literature in 1923. Yeats was deeply involved with esoteric activities in his time and a well-known figure in the Theosophical Movement. For Yeats the Sidhe were not just mythical creatures but living realities. He often referred to them and several of his well-known poems describe the Sidhe or the Faery People, or simply Faeries as he also called them. Among them it is important to mention *The Hosting of the Sidhe, A Faery Song, The Song of Wandering Aengus,* the play *The Land of Heart's Desire* and—not the least—*The Stolen Child,* one of the most famous Irish poems. Yeats was saturated by the Irish mythology, especially in his younger years, and to him the Sidhe were not fantasies but living beings amongst us. There is much to unfold when his Sidhe-poems are investigated, also regarding places where Sidhe-encounters took place.

Yeats had a very special friend, to a certain degree standing in his shadow, but who was a prominent figure in the Celtic, Irish

Renaissance. His name was George William Russell (1867–1935), but he is more widely known under his artist synonym "AE" (or Æ), signifying "Aeon" as he considered his greater, timeless being to be the true source of his most inspired work. AE is a gentle giant and his significance in newer Irish history is considerable. He is known as a writer, editor and critic who found many new cultural talents. He was also an agricultural pioneer who fought for the Irish farmers and Irish independence. Just like Yeats he was involved with Theosophy but must importantly he was a poet in his own right, a painter and a seer who had many and vivid encounters with angels, nature spirits and not the least the Sidhe—and he knew the difference between them. He wrote about his encounters in his autobiography, *The Candle of Vision*, and many of his paintings show how the Sidhe appeared to him.

AE was a mystic in his own right, and the effect he had on others as a wise man is a story in itself. It must have been a very special experience to have such a significant, cultural and spiritual pioneer sharing intimate, spiritual visions in the beginning of the 20th century. His paintings invite us into his contacts in an intimate way, and poems like *On a Hillside, The Dream of the Children, The Call of the Sidhe, A New World* and several others echo the haunting beauty, uplifting joy and majestic grandeur he was experiencing with the Sidhe. When he was able to, he liked to withdraw to Donegal in Northern Ireland where he wrote poems and painted in the area of Marble Hill Beach, Dunfanaghy and Mount Muckish—one of the sacred mountains called The Seven Sisters. He even had his own place, known as Fairy Cottage, where he spent much time. A deeper study into the work of AE is a rare opening into the Irish world of the Sidhe.

Not Angels, Devas, or Nature Spirits

A very relevant question arises from the theme of the Sidhe: How is it possible at all to distinguish between the many differing entities inhabiting the subtle realm bordering our physical world? As most people don't even believe in their existence, it seems to be quite a task to sort things out. First, it must be emphasized that several gifted clairvoyant pioneers have been investigating these areas for more than a century, and they portray their encounters in very similar ways. It is not theoretical speculations but perceptions that lay the ground for the present evidence available to us. Scientific proofs following the current procedures will not lead to a public acceptance of angels and other beings now, but evidence based on observations are piling up and today's belief may become tomorrow's knowledge. Before trying to distinguish the species or types of beings, I want to honor some of the trailblazers that have paved the way to what we can access today.

Besides the observations of AE (George William Russell), it is pertinent to mention the pioneering work of Dora van Gelder Kunz (1904-1999) and especially Geoffrey Hodson (1886-1983), two eminent clairvoyant investigators in the 20th century. Dora's book *The Real World of Fairies: A First-Person Account*, from 1937 was a brave, early investigation. Geoffrey Hodson spent almost 60 years investigating angels, devas and nature spirits and his monumental works, *The Kingdom of the Gods* and *Clairvoyant Investigations* constitute a powerful evidence of this, but a range of his books give a wealth of insight into these subtle realms. His earliest works in these areas date back to around 1925.

In recent decades Dorothy Maclean (1920–2020) and her primary role in co-founding the Findhorn Community in Northern Scotland speaks for itself, as this world-famous project, initiated in 1962 by Peter and Eileen Caddy and herself, essentially was established from a living collaboration between angels, devas, nature spirits and humans. Dorothy's works, *To Hear the Angels Sing,* and *Call of the Trees* are beautiful examples of the nature of her inner contacts. David Spangler needs no further introduction. However, his involvement in the development of Findhorn is important to include, and his more than 50 books are a true treasure house. His recent works, *Conversations with the Sidhe, Engaging with the Sidhe,* and *Subtle Worlds,* are of special interest in this context, together with the manual to *The Sidhe*

Card Deck, co-authored with Jeremy Berg. Lorian Association, the organization he co-founded with his wife Julia and others, has close relations to Findhorn and in recent years, after careful consideration, David has included the Sidhe as part of the Incarnational Spirituality that constitutes the core of the Lorian curriculum.

There are many other sources, including the spiritual teacher and author, Peter Dawkins, from England who I cooperated with years back and learnt a lot from, and Eskild Tjalve, a good Danish colleague that has also investigated clairvoyantly into the nature of devas, angels and nature spirits. Several more around the globe could be included. I want to honor those that have had a special impact on me and the path I walk.

An attempt to summarize the related and differing nature of devas, angels, nature spirits, humans and the Sidhe is difficult, as there will be so many generalizations that tend to eliminate the countless variations and differing features. Extensive books have been written about all the differing aspects of these beings. Bear this in mind in the following which is a brief attempt to paint a very broad and general picture of vast and multifaceted realms.

THE HUMAN KINGDOM

For a moment, let's look at ourselves. We humans incarnate in a physical, organic body in the dense, physical world. We have a lifespan of normally less than 100 years. When we die, we let go of the body and return it to the Gaian ecology, as we assimilate the experiences in the subtle worlds and prepare for another physical chapter on our long life-journey of awakening. Due to the conditions in the dense, physical reality, our consciousness is skilled in perceiving differences and duality. We learn to discern and analyze in small details and it is normal for us to contrast things and to experience a "right and wrong" or a "bad and good" as we propel ourselves through the heavy reality of survival. The outer experiences have made us focus almost entirely on the phenomena of surface existence and we tend to accept only tangible aspects of totality as real. This is a fair description of at least the present consciousness dominating the world.

We mainly create in solid, physical forms while we have a creative consciousness with much more capacity. Slowly we are awakening to the greater reality of life. We are incredibly different in cultures and our lives as women or men have many colors and nuances, making human life a multifaceted reality full of immense potential. Gradually we learn to unfold the free will and our innermost treasure is our precious capacity to love. Now we are experiencing many crises due to our present stage of evolution and greed, fear and isolation play a significant role in our present situation as we have not yet—as a species—awakened to our spiritual nature.

We live as one species amongst many on the planet, and yet we tend to dominate, use and exploit other species as we perceive ourselves to be the most important and intelligent of them all. This mentality has created many problems for us, and now we are taking hard lessons in learning a much humbler approach towards our fellow species. As we have challenged the planet, so the planet challenges us and the great wake-up call in our time is the need to stop the exploitation of the planet and make us start respecting the dignity and rights of other species from animals, birds, fish and insects to plants, minerals, microbes and other life forms that are part of the Gaian ecology. From there we can continue respecting other species that are not physical as ourselves, but equally part of the inner Gaian ecology. Still, we are an incredibly dominating species, forcing our own standards upon all life. It is a hard process for us to start waking up to greater humility and awareness.

THE DEVA KINGDOM

Speaking in general, devas or angels are names referring to the same kingdom or reality. However, there are usually distinctions made as this vast realm has many different aspects. It slightly differs how people differentiate between devas and angels, but devas mostly relate to beings closely connected to nature while angels seem to be associated with functions or qualities not necessarily focused in nature. However, this distinction is not completely accurate but only point at a tendency in the way terms are used. Devas or angels are not incarnated in the way we are, but they do have forms of manifestation in the subtle worlds of varying density. They can express themselves all the way down to the physical reality, but only in the most etheric frequencies. They manifest in bodies of energy that are less dense than our human organic expressions or what we see around us in dense, physical nature. They precipitate into mental, emotional and etheric matter and express their life in a living flow. Part of their energies expands out and the formations have been interpreted as wings, but they do not fly like birds. They move swiftly if needed but can also hold fixed positions for extensive periods. Often, they have responsibilities lasting for centuries or thousands of years at the same place.

Angels or devas perceive the life-force and the purpose behind outer phenomena. Their consciousness creates energetic designs molding outer forms and many of them are the architects and form-builders behind the living manifestations of nature. Contact with devas or angels tend to have a universal characteristic. It is not personal in the way we are accustomed to. Normally the atmosphere is full of joy and upliftment like a fountain of light. The universal touch is more like meeting a nature force than it is a personal chat about private details. One should not expect a deva or an angel to be interested in our human society as such, with all the peculiar human characteristics we take for granted. These beings are usually not that close to our daily doings, except for the few who have learnt about our customs and characteristics. Their sense of time is also very different from ours. Their lifespan is radically different as they can use the same, vibrating energy-field for thousands of years. Their evolution is slow but steady and with no drama like we know it. When the time comes and their tasks are fulfilled, they withdraw from their denser expression, until another opportunity of development makes them precipitate again in other forms.

They often appear as colorful figures or forms, surrounded by a large energy field, extending far from them and creating an atmosphere saturated with their qualities. Some are more feminine and others more masculine, yet most of them appear more androgyne and they are not divided in gender as we. Some of them are remote from Humanity and barely detect our existence, while others are closer to us. Some of these learn to communicate with us, and because of this fact angels or devas have been considered to be subtle helpers in our lives. They have numerous responsibilities and it is a huge theme covered in many books. They evolve a self-consciousness like we humans, but it is not in their nature to act individually and independent as their consciousness is deeply embedded in the universal flow of life. They are expressions of the natural laws, both outer and inner, and to them it is usually not an option to act in isolation.

The multitudes of nature spirits belong to this vast kingdom and beings like undines, gnomes, goblins, fairies, dryads, sylphs, salamanders and many other names refer to different nature spirits that finally evolve into devas or angels. There is a kind of similarity here to how animals and other species in the physical world evolve into what we could call the human kingdom or a realm resembling the human consciousness. The nature spirits act from a more instinctive intelligence and they do not possess self-consciousness like ours. Contact with them is an immediate in-the-moment-encounter that often gives an enhanced experience of the richness of nature.

THE SIDHE KINGDOM

We are used to talking about different planes and worlds from a certain perspective, placing us in the central region. Spiritual and esoteric traditions tend to describe realms as degrees of denseness, layered almost on the top of each other. This is the central sight perspective, the view of layered denseness. The Sidhe experience things from a somewhat different perspective. Compared to us they live in the peripheral regions of energy or matter. They are not—at least to us—centered in a clearly defined world of particles like we perceive it, but much more as part of a world of fields with less sharp distinctions. David has used the picture that the Sidhe live in a stem cell reality, whereas we are evolving as specialized cells. Because of this difference the Sidhe experience much more flow and effortless shapeshifting, if needed. This is one of the reasons why they seem to fascinate us so much. Because of their plasticity and flowing conditions, the Sidhe easily relate to the deva kingdom, and as they are affected by their contacts, some of them even resemble angels, devas or even nature spirits to a certain degree and have been experienced as such by human observers.

The Sidhe also incarnate in mental, emotional and etheric matter, but mainly in the peripheral regions of these realms. They are female and male like us and they give birth to children like we do. Their civilization on Earth is very diversified and the functions of the Sidhe are also very differentiated. They utilize their energetic bodies in much more fluid and flexible conditions and they can shapeshift in ways we find magical. Their consciousness mainly perceives connections and wholeness and they primarily create via their imagination in mental and emotional matter. The Sidhe are our closest relatives and in our ancient past we were one species. They normally live in the same form for centuries and there are reports of Sidhe who are more than two thousand years old and still in the same body. These conditions are partly due to the flexibility and regenerative capacities of their realm and consciousness. There are fewer Sidhe than humans in total, but they constitute a large species anyway and their impact on the Gaian wholeness is significant.

The Sidhe never lose their sense of wholeness and flow and because of this their consciousness is very different from ours. They have self-consciousness as we, but the deep sense of connectedness makes conditions and life-expressions very different from ours. They do not tend to rebel against given structures—at least not like we tend to do. They develop much more organically and gradual than we and because of this the pace of their evolution seems to be slower than ours. From our perspective the Sidhe are magical beings and they live up to this because they have deep insight into the transformative possibilities of energy and being. They live in an awareness that can inspire us to renewal and remind us of our shared past—our inner Sidhe nature and their inner Human seed. The Sidhe are characterized by a presence full of peace and at the same time deeply attuned to the moods and expressions of nature and landscapes. Encountering them gives a sense of a wild and untamed presence, but deeply rooted and full of peaceful connectedness at the same time.

Not all Sidhe find us humans attractive. In fact, many of them consider us to be very dangerous and who can blame them? They sense our impact on the planet and perceive the destructive aspects of our doings. Because of this it is not all Sidhe who find it attractive to connect with us and they are not united in this effort. There is deep concern amongst them about the prospects and there is a real risk in the present attempts to cooperate with us. However, it seems that the groups of Sidhe who endeavor in the new agenda are growing and there are signs of upliftment, judging from many of the new ways it inspires people.

The Children of Gaia

There is another evolution that sometimes get confused with the Sidhe. This realm has been called many things, including Faery beings or Fae. Here I refer to them as *the Children of Gaia* or *the Kingdom of Pan*. They are deeply connected with the subconscious nature of our planet, or Gaia, and express the dreaming playfulness of the planetary life. Some of them have been portrayed as the fabled creatures of the past and as strange mixtures of beings. Their consciousness is deeply instinctual and collective in ways that seem strange to us. They are so deeply embedded in the nature form of Gaia that, at least to us, suggest their consciousness seems to be below the physical threshold and not above. They can be extremely flexible in their form-expressions and are eminent shapeshifters. Some of them appear as creatures resembling mythical beings portrayed in different human traditions, and quite a few of them are what we would call fauns or satyrs. Sometimes their looks can resemble nature spirits, the Sidhe or even we humans, but their consciousness is entirely different, almost inaccessible to us, and deeply instinctual and amoral. Later I will give an example of one encounter of this kind, as it may help distinguishing between the Sidhe and the Children of Gaia.

Guardians of the Portals

Many traditions connect the Sidhe with sacred places, mounds, trees, stone circles and ancient places in nature, and there is relevant truth in these claims. There have always been connections between

Humanity and the Sidhe realm, no matter how much it has been cloaked in traits of superstition, misunderstandings and fear. Real encounters have been existing all the time. Partly because of this, sacred places—especially those connected with nature—have been used as gateways for the Sidhe to connect between their world and ours. The Sidhe realm borders to our physical world. There are strong links at some of the places where we live, and there are great areas in undisturbed nature where the Sidhe realm is very close to our nature. Because of this it is possible to invite a connection when we are physically at such places. It is not a must, but an obvious possibility.

As already mentioned, in Ireland the Sidhe tradition is particularly strong and there are many places known to be Sidhe areas and focal points for lore and stories of humans contacting the Sidhe or vice versa. It is said that the legendary harpist, Turloch O'Carolan (1670–1738), who was born blind, connected with the Sidhe in nature and even got access to their inner places through mounds and hills where he lived. From this connection he got some of his most famous tunes. Many places in Ireland have legends and lore connected with the Sidhe, Ben Bulben being one of them and considered to be a huge Fairy Fort. The huge, flat-topped rock formation in County Sligo is an impressive sight and a massive presence. If one follows in the footsteps of Yeats and AE, there will be a treasure of places alone in NW Ireland to discover and learn from. It is not the place here to list uncountable places of interest as it would take up all the space. Suffice to say that there are lots of wonderful places, not only in Ireland, but all over the world, that are focal points for connecting with the Sidhe. Google a few minutes and you will see for yourself. Besides places made by humans, there are many places in nature known to be Sidhe portals themselves.

The Sidhe do some of their activities where sacred places like stone circles, monoliths, mounds and other types of focal points have been established thousands of years back, and they have similar activities at certain places in nature that can be found and experienced. The Sidhe are guardians of portals and for ages they have specialized in bridging worlds. Sometimes stories tell of important encounters at such places, and some of my own meetings with Fjeldur have occurred at key-places where the atmosphere was concentrated. This is important to mention as it can become an inspiring journey of discoveries. There is research here for more than a lifetime and at a personal level it can be significant to know this as there might be a natural attraction to certain places and possible sites to visit. I encourage openness towards this.

The important thing here is not to give the impression that Sidhe contact can only occur at sacred sites or in special places in nature. David Spangler had his first contact on a sofa in his living room and his home continues to be the main place for his encounters with the Sidhe. My own first distinct contact was in a guest room where I slept during a workshop I held in Northern Jutland, and I have had several inspirations from him while sitting at cafes or in public places in cities. It would be a mistake to believe that Sidhe contact requires specific locations and a rare timing. It can literally happen anywhere and at any time. In the end, it is all a matter of intention, heart and mind. Having said that, do give yourself the opportunity to visit special places and to attune to the Sidhe while being in nature. It surely is a wonderful help. Being in nature is always a possible catalyzer for contact as they are so deeply attuned to the green heartbeat of Gaia and with the living world of nature and its stunning beauty.

When we are in nature we also tend to relax more and let go of business as usual. We breathe more freely and experience the world we have not molded entirely from our own ideas. Seek out tranquility and regeneration where there are trees, flowers, running water, hills and the rejuvenating elements of nature. Find out where you most easily attune and investigate what it does with you and how you are affected. There is a probability that you may be encountered in some way or another by one of the Sidhe guardians in nature. Nevertheless, do not forget that you and I in ourselves constitute the most important portals for contact. If we are not properly attuned, we may visit as many places we want to, and most likely nothing at all will happen. *Portals are made by consciousness bridging worlds.*

ᴑ GIFT ᴐ
Heaven—Earth—Heart

Give yourself the gift of inviting to be a portal by a very simple activity.
I call it Heaven-Earth-Heart as it is an opening through these three
aspects of ourselves. Find an undisturbed place and a good time to
do this. It can be done sitting—or lying—but I recommend you do
it standing.

Stand relaxed and close your eyes. Breathe naturally and connect
with your whole body. Relax and sense how it is to stand physically.
Connect with your feelings and relax emotionally. Allow yourself to
experience a natural calmness. Relax and sense how it is to stand
emotionally. Connect with your mind and relax mentally. Allow
yourself to experience that you observe your thoughts but do not
engage with them right now. Relax and sense how it is to stand fully
awakened in your whole being.

Honor yourself personally as a human being and stand relaxed
in your sovereignty—honor your humanity. Honor that you are a
fragment of the universe, expressing yourself as human, with full
dignity and in your uniqueness. Realize that you are always potentially a bridge between heaven and earth. You are a living bridge.

Open yourself to the mighty heaven above, the sky that always
holds and surrounds you. If it feels right, you can raise your arms
and reach for the sky. Open yourself to the light of the Sun and to
the glittering stars shining in infinite space. Stand under the majesty
of heaven and open yourself to receive the solar light and the clarity
of the glittering stars. Receive the gentle downpour from above. As a
slow-motion shower, let the sparkling star light and glowing sunlight
pour gently down through you. Become a living stargate and receive
it down through your whole body from above to below. Receive the
glittering, glowing light.

As the light from above passes through you, let it descend into the
Earth and connect deeply with the mighty Mother Earth below, the
deep ground that always holds you and nurtures you. If it feels right,

you can crouch down and let your hands touch the Earth below. Open yourself to the deep peace and support from below, and from the light of the Earth, coming from the very heart of Gaia at the center of the Globe. Receive the rising peace and nurturing care from the Earth below you and sense the nectar of the bountiful Earth, rising and regenerating you from below. As a slow-motion upliftment, let the renewing peace and life from Mother Earth permeate your body and being. Become a living Earth gate and receive it up through you, as the living Earth nectar through you ascends to heaven above.

Sense your warm, gentle, light-filled heart in your very center as a meeting place for starlight and Earth-nectar. In your Heart you become the Heart of Stars and Earth—you are filled with gentle presence and let it emanate through you as a gift to everything around you. If it feels right, you can hold your hands over your breast and connect with the mildness in you. Slowly open your eyes and offer the star-nectar of Heaven-Earth-Heart to everything around you. Offer it as a gift as you honor and appreciate everything around you. If it feels right, you can open your arms and hands in an embrace of everything around you.

Gradually return to your daily doings, refreshed and aligned. Take a little time to connect with the energy and atmosphere generated by the small ritual of Heaven-Earth-Heart you have just practiced.

Dancers in the Land

The Sidhe are deeply anchored in the land where they are, and by their very being they are portals between worlds in an almost effortless way. Symbolically they are standing stones in the vast connectedness of the kingdom of Gaia. They never lose the sense of being part of everything around them. They are so deeply rooted in the land that they become the land and wear nature as their garment. Isolation is a foreign country to them, an alienation they do not easily relate to. They sense the sacredness of everything around them and the aliveness of matter as light-filled energy is natural to them. In their world everything seems to respond with aliveness in an instant. Constant renewal is just as natural to them as habitual repetition is to us. In making the Sidhe Card Deck Jeremy and David were asked to focus on the stones and the dancers as the dynamic opposites that merge and live in the Sidhe. Anchoring or being the standing stone blends with movement or the living dancer, and wholeness is the basic Sidhe nature. Becoming the stone and the dancer at the same time enables the "in-betweenness" to emerge, and life becomes full of living portals between worlds.

David has used a beautiful picture to describe this. The sea anemone is firmly rooted with its trunk and attached to a hard surface by its base, while its many tentacles move gracefully in the flow of the waters in the sea. The Sidhe are symbolical sea anemones, connecting with the deep base of Gaia while weaving energies in the gigantic sea of connectedness. A similar picture I have received on numerous occasions is the tree and the wind. Deeply rooted in the earth, the tree is standing with its vertical trunk while stretching its branches and leaves out in the open air and in persistent movement by the living winds. Or the dynamic interplay can be experienced as a wind-harp, letting the music emerge from the resonance between the tense strings of the stable instrument and the living breeze in the air.

The Sidhe-nature can only blossom in complete freedom, in natural wildness. Exactly the sense of wildness is so prevalent in encountering anything concerning the Sidhe. Not a blind wildness—a conscious wildness exhibiting the features of untamedness, an unattached awareness that has often been described as almost feral, and yet not predatory in any way. Compared to us the Sidhe are undomesticated and seem unfettered from so many things we are attached to. In South American shamanism there is a word for this, *Salka*. Salka has been described as the wild wind that blows through our world of conventions and norms, calling us to rediscover the beauty of all things and the great mystery of life. Salka is under the stars and supported by the fragrant earth. Salka is the natural state of wildness we all come from, and the undomesticated identity we all have inherited but almost entirely forgotten. The Sidhe are Guardians of Salka, they are constant reminders of that which we need to rediscover.

Singers of Living Imagination

We are endowed with a voice—and it can speak and sing. We humans talk a lot. The Sidhe are born singers. They live in a realm full of life-musicality because they sense the rhythms, the melodies and the harmonies in everything. This is the normality of their world, and they brim with singing in all its diverse and multicolored ways. Singing does not mean standing in a choir or performing from a scene. It means weaving, connecting and creating in all activities. All that exists is a grand symphony and all creatures add their tunes to the manifestation. This is the world of the Sidhe. Their breath is a song. They live in flow, flux and frolic. As Fjeldur's intention states in my interpretation:

> "The stone and the dancer can also be called the tree and the wind, or the mountain and the butterfly. As shamans or creative dreamers, we must stand deeply rooted in ourselves and in the depth of Gaia with the upright trunk and the crown stretching up towards Cosmos. Here we can sense the living movements of the wind and let it sing through our nature. The tree and the wind coming together creates the song, and as singers we listen to the wind and become its living instruments. It dances in the trees, and the song is the new being woven in the union of the two. The shaman, the creative dreamer or the dragon rider is the standing power riding imagination, and interpreting its nature and message through deep connection with the living tunes of dance and song."

In our world we have a mythical story reminding us about our ancient past. It is the story about Orpheus. According to legend his mother was a muse and as Apollo gave him a lyre the muses taught him to play it. Apollon was surprised as no one could resist his singing and playing. The most famous part of his deeds is not that he was one of the Argonauts and helped to capture the Golden Fleece in Colchis.

It is the story about how he was married to Eurydice who died, and how he was allowed to descend to Hades to get her back. The story about their love is a tale of the loss and how he almost got her but looked for her in the last seconds and lost her completely as he broke the oath not to look back. This is the archetypal story of human love, of separation, loss and grief. However, the story about his singing and playing is the Sidhe-part of his nature. It is said that Orpheus enchanted all living beings when he played his lyre and sang. Animals came together in groups and listened. Conflicting parts stopped their quarrel. Trees and cliffs changed their position and created forma-tions. Even the rivers changed their course and the Gods themselves listened and sometimes wept.

The lyre is the origin to being lyrical, and Orpheus is a living example of how we have the Sidhe nature within us. Orpheus is a true hero and one of the legendary Argonauts that Jason assembled for his epic journey. He shows the human story of love, loss and heartache. However, he also demonstrates the human Sidhe story of the magic of song and music that make everything alive and responding. So, Orpheus is both human and Sidhe and he reminds us of a shared past. In the words of Shakespeare:

"Orpheus with his lute made trees,
And the mountain tops that freeze,
Bow themselves when he did sing:
To his music plants and flowers
Ever sprung; as sun and showers
There had made a lasting spring.
Everything that heard him play,
Even the billows of the sea,
Hung their heads, and then lay by.
In sweet music is such art,
Killing care and grief of heart
Fall asleep, or hearing, die."
Henry VIII, Act III, scene 1

The Sidhe live in a reality we have almost lost. They breathe and move in the winds that play on the harp of life in everything. We humans are taught and trained to be logical while the Sidhe are lyrical. *The stuff that dreams are made of*—Prospero's words in Shakespeare's *The Tempest* (Act IV, scene 1) is the source of all song, namely imagination. The Sidhe in their world draw on imagination and make it into song—or they create from it. But what does this mean?

For we humans, imagination is something subjective. It is something we create in our private minds. It is something we fabricate out of our own substance. It is a subjective activity and not what we would consider to be real. For the Sidhe imagination is objective. They live in it. They experience imagination as a living substance that they can partner with. The Sidhe would say that they are imagination personified. David Spangler shares a beautiful and illustrative image from his female Sidhe contact, Mariel. If we consider the Sidhe to be creatures, that never left the sea, we humans did so, and we carry with us the water in our bodies. If we see the water as the substance of imagination, the creative forces, the Sidhe live in the element and it is the substance of their world, while we carry it with us and imagination to us is something individual as we create our own, inner worlds. Each situation is unique and gives certain opportunities.

The Sidhe live in a much more collective or shared world of imagination with coherency and community, different to humans. They share a "field-imagination" much more than we who are in the realm of more isolated "particle-imagination." We humans have developed a much more distinct ability to create individual worlds. Within our confines we have personalized imagination. We experience a more explicit, fragmented or confined imagination. Both the field and the particle have their significance, and yet wholeness embrace both, so there is mutual learning at hand.

Imagination is also the quality of matter that makes shapeshifting possible. We humans can shapeshift, but to a lesser degree and with clear limits. When we change in mood it can be seen in our faces and the way we carry ourselves. If we dramatically change our diet it can also be seen as time goes when we gain or lose weight. The Sidhe can mold their form in an instant if needed. This does not mean that they do it constantly and it depends on their chosen path. Shapeshifting is the very nature of life in movement and we humans tend to get stuck in routines while our Sidhe relatives breathe much more in flux and flow. In this way their world is more open than ours, and yet, we can manifest in a more solid denseness than they can, so again a new partnership is an untested adventure. Fjeldur's sharing in my words:

"Creation is song, and the song is danced into form. The living portal—the Sidhe Shaman—rides the dragon of creative imagination, winding its way through the living landscape, following the pulse which is the song of all that lives, the very meaning or purpose of everything, and creating new wholeness. I am a singer and as Sidhe-singer I chant to you and invite you to dance life into new forms. The dance is in everything and becomes alive in everything when it is sung—the song that is the breeze of spirit in the trees. Stand up as trees and be soft in the crowns so the airstream can play in your hair and let the smile come forth in your wild faces and blameless nature. Be wild with us, with smiling warmth, so we can stand and be moved as the creative dancers, singing the songs of the new winds—the songs that have been melancholic memories of long-gone ages and lost magic, and now can become new revelations of ecstasy."

You and I are potentially dragon riders on the flow of imagination. As the Sidhe we can learn to follow ancient song-lines and to create new ones. Song-lines are the living threads that connect everything. Listening to them is to read the living stories of life and resounding them is vitalizing the world of Gaia. Creating new song-lines is to become creative in the vast world we are part of. When the Sidhe do this, they always deeply attune to wholeness, so the new creation is an embedded part of wholeness, and not an isolated thing. They literally sing things into being in a meditative attunement to the larger landscape.

David has shared a single Sidhe word that Mariel, his Sidhe contact, wanted to communicate. The word is *Anwa*, and the reality behind it plays a central role in the Sidhe realm. Learning a little about it is learning about something of immense significance, not the least to us humans. Anwa implies purpose and connectedness at the same time. Mariel would call Anwa the real form or activity of anything. Anwa is the living function of any being, and at its deepest level it is the moving pattern of spirit. Anwa is about form and activity at the same time. All sentient beings have an inner purpose, a driving impulse, that is destined to be expressed in outer activity. When this is accomplished, there is harmony added to the greater wholeness of life. Anwa is all about identity, and to the Sidhe nothing is isolated, so identity is the particle and the field at the same time—it is individuality and fellowship united.

Our true "form" is our innermost life-purpose expressed together with the core-drive of others. It is when we sing our Soul-song and dance our Soul-dance together with others. It is the doing that comes from our being—and it is a joined togetherness where each singing dancer is part of the greater choir and dancing company. This living expression is always part of true joy, so, to sense Anwa we need to look for joy and the living togetherness. It is the form of my song and how I sing it with others. It is the skills I cherish most and how I blend them in cooperation with others. It is the way I am me, truly me, and deeply connected with my greater sense of belonging and being part of a "we."

Nothing seems to be more important than this, and it highlights why connecting with the Sidhe can be a catalyzer for our own awakening. It also shows that our Sidhe relatives have something valuable to learn from us. Their crystal bright hearts and our warm compassion. Their connective flow and our manifesting power. Their fields and our particles. Their lyrical glee and our penetrating logic. Their frolic dance and our funny walk. The joint exploration and journey of wonders has just begun.

The Card Deck of the Sidhe

My friend Jeremy Berg, who has dedicated a great deal of his time and energy to co-creation with the Sidhe, has created a wonderful tool of connection with the Sidhe. Together with David Spangler and following guidance from their Sidhe contacts, he has manifested the now widely used 55 cards known as *The Sidhe Card Deck*. Its basic structure is characterized by stone-cards, dancer-cards and additional Grail-cards, and they all revolve around a central Mound or Howe, the archetypal energy behind the word Sidhe and many traditions around the sacred Mounds and stone circles. I warmly recommend the card deck as a helping tool to focus on key qualities of the Sidhe and our own inner Sidhe-nature, and there is much inspiration and insight to get from it. Here Jeremy shares how the call to create the cards not only opened him to immense inspiration, but actually also made him come forth as an artist:

"The Card Deck of the Sidhe has been my primary tool for connection and collaboration with the Sidhe. Prior to the creation of the deck I had never been a painter. This all changed when one day a male Sidhe appeared behind me in my office in Everett, WA and described in detail an image of what became the central card in the deck, the Howe. At the time I did not know what a 'Howe' was or even that several existed as actual, megalithic remnants of a bygone culture throughout Europe and beyond. I became a painter trying to describe the vision that was given. Here is my original painting alongside an actual Howe on the Welsh island of Anglesey. Interestingly this Howe, Bryn Celli Ddu, was once surrounded by a stone circle (as was Newgrange in Ireland). This became the structure of the card deck as described to David Spangler a few days later by a female Sidhe companion of my visitor.

"What followed this initial contact was a series of—for me—mostly evening contacts in which an image for a card along with

**The Howe from the
Card Deck of the Sidhe**

**Entrance to
Bryn Celli Ddu, Anglesey**

an imbedded meaning would flash into my mind. This is described in the manual for the deck along with David's experiences building the deck.

"I could also feel the presence of the Sidhe while painting and they have always been supportive of my workshops, frequently offering new insights and stories.

"So, the Card Deck of the Sidhe is a practical, imaginal tool to make contact with the Sidhe. That contact may announce itself to you through the synchronicities of the card deck and the attendant wave of inspiration, information and emotion or in some other way.

"But the Sidhe are not limited to the card deck or telepathic engagement. They can appear through your love and connection to nature and the land as an overall felt sense of joy and beauty. You may feel their presence on the wild wind or in your dreams. They may join you while you dance or sing or create in other ways.

"Invite their presence through an open heart and love for our beautiful earth, yourself, each other, and for the Sidhe and they will respond in ways unique to you and your sensibilities.

"May all your collaborations with the Sidhe offer a blessing to you, to them, to nature and to the larger Gaian life we share."

↺ GIFT ↻
The New Call

Give yourself the gift of finding a time and place to wonder about what is stirring in you, right now in your life. Not tomorrow and a year ahead and at another place. Right now. Right here. Relax and open your mind and feelings to the heartland within you. The gentle heart of open space in your very center. The place in you that is always intimately embraced and united with your relaxed breathing. The lightness behind everything heavy. The open sky and the fragrant earth in you. Take a little time to sense this, almost like a fragrance, a scent of tender, open space.

Ask yourself: How do I sense a new call in my life? What is calling from within? What brings up joy in me, pure joy and affirmation? What is emerging in me as an almost silent note of hope and delight?

Ask yourself: How can I nurture the flame of hope and joy and wonder in my life? What can I partner with, so I am not isolated in my longing for enjoyment and life-unfoldment? Where is my place of joy in life?

Allow yourself to taste this like something delicious, to touch it with care and tenderness. Give your daily mind a vacation and stretch your imagination up and down and in and out. Let go of any sense of "living-up-to" and "performing-optimal" and "deserving." What is deep inside you is a sprouting seed from your natural, undisturbed wildness. Let it move. Let it move you. Let yourself be moved. What is the new call in you? Stretch out your hand and connect with it. How is your response to the call?

2

CLOSE ENCOUNTERS

Why Engage?

It seems fair to ask the question: Why should we engage with the Sidhe? We have plenty on our plate already, and why complicate a demanding situation with even more challenges? We humans have great difficulties in even tolerating each other and we are in many conflicts in a challenged world, so why bother? Why engage into a strange exploration into realms far from our everyday life? These questions are legitimate and understandable.

First, if we take such an approach, we can dismiss innumerable other things in a similar way. Why try to learn a difficult skill? We have difficulties enough already. Why explore strange things? We have problems all over in our modern world that demand more attention. So, the reason we might engage must come from another angle. The fact that we live in challenging times and confront issues in our daily living that puts pressure on us, makes such an engagement even more relevant. Here is how it can be presented:

We should only engage with the Sidhe if it seems to be relevant, meaningful and helpful to a better life. Engaging with the Sidhe is not a matter of pure curiosity, escape from daily living or getting lost in a never-never land. On the contrary. Engaging should come from a place in us that yearns for more wholeness, for loving relationships and for new opportunities in living a creative life manifesting goodness, beauty and growth. *The deepest call from the Sidhe is a call to wholeness, a call to heal the divisions and the separation that cause pain, ignorance and a lack of ability to unfold in life. Their reaching out is carried on a wave of vision and hope that building bridges and relating is much better and richer for all than remaining in isolation and lack of flow, not just for us, but for the planetary life.*

Seen with a bird's eye perspective the call of the Sidhe is the call of Gaia to bring the living beings together in a growing, living wholeness. It is a peace call, and it is an appeal to all of us that we should start appreciating our mutual co-existence and start the journey of learning to co-create together in the larger realm of the living planet. From an even more serious perspective we could say that it is urgently important that we reconnect with our deepest roots in the ancestry we share. The two divided branches need to re-join. Isolated and divided we will less likely succeed in making the home of Gaia into a harmonious wholeness. They come forth—in a way—as a call from Gaia herself, urging us to reunite the family.

If we take this big perspective and put it into an eye to eye perspective, it is all about creating good neighborship. After all, the Sidhe are called *The Good Neighbors* and why should we not become part of that equation? Living with good relations to neighbors opens up a much richer and joyful life—not in isolation, superstition, gossip and fear, but in mutual helpfulness, enhanced life-quality and deeper connectedness with the world in all its aspects. It might be the fact that some of we humans have difficulties in appreciating our differences, but that should not shut the door for all others that desire to engage with differences and multiplicity. The Sidhe-Human relationship is all about family reunion as it is about good neighborship. From this, innumerable things will emerge, and it is an endeavor worth making. The time has come to start making this happening and those of us who feel the call are certainly invited on the journey.

A Healthy Approach

It is easy to fall into the trap of glamor and claim-making, and to create the devotional dependence and worshipping climate that hinders a healthy partnership between the Sidhe and us. We must avoid these immature regressions and stand forth in a truly progressive and mature spirit of responsible cooperation and a real friendship based upon mutuality and genuine respect. This is what the Sidhe repeatedly have asked of us, and we should live up to it, and not fall back to the ways of the past.

A good approach seems to be starting with openness and also with a curious mind able to handle anything regarding the Sidhe in the same spirit as with everything else. We are asked to stand in our human dignity and from a position of sovereignty and kindness we can invite fellowship and cooperation. We should never take the position as humble receivers of lofty messages. It only creates an uneven and unbalanced relationship. The Sidhe are not above us. They are with us. We can create a solid foundation for a healthy approach when we combine standing in our own natural authority with a sober clarity and a good sense of humor. The Sidhe do have humor, and they want to approach us in a spirit of equality and harmony. If we establish a well-balanced atmosphere in our willingness and sincere interest in engaging with our *Good Neighbors*, there is a good chance of a fruitful outcome.

The Room, the Activity, and the Contact

Quite a few people tend to put expectations high and to hope for deep encounters. At the same time the ambition seems to make it very difficult to live up to the lofty standards set by the eager mind and the longing. Making Sidhe contact into a performance target is not a very balanced start. So, how can we relate to making a possible contact in a relaxed way? Simply by tuning in to the Sidhe frequency—already described—and by inviting a warm relationship in a mutual caring for Gaia and all living beings. How might we sense that something is actually happening? I suggest a path consisting of three elements: The room, the activity and the contact.

First, we have the room. This simply means that after inviting the Sidhe for a contact, we can be aware of an atmosphere, a certain climate or environment that might become present. The first time I experienced anything relating to the Sidhe it was a sensing of the Sidhe realm as such, somewhat resembling the feeling you may have when you enter a room or sense a room close to you with its own distinctive quality. Think of standing in a hall and sensing a living room with an open door. You might get a feeling of a distinct ambience. Or think of being in nature, standing at a gate and looking into a valley that is a world of its own. You can pick up something although you are not totally there. This is what I call sensing the room. It is a registering of the Sidhe realm or the Sidhe field in a general sense. Leaning into this might be the first way of sensing a kind of contact.

Secondly, you might discover at a certain point that there is something going on in the neighboring room. There is distinct activity. Now, what characterizes this activity? What qualities does it have? Does it carry a fragrance, does it carry sounds, sensations or colors? Does it have a distinct disposition or mood? Let your natural interest open to it. Do you experience a general activity, or does it relate to you in ways you are gradually becoming aware of? Exploring and diving into the room and its activity is a good way of becoming aware of the Sidhe realm. At the same time, it might stir something within you. It may stimulate your own inner Sidhe nature making you open yourself to the living rhythms and musicality from your deeply rooted connectedness to wholeness. This in itself will make it easier for the Sidhe to come by and say hello in a natural way.

Thirdly, there is the contact itself. It will come if it is relevant and if you are able to perceive it consciously. Don't expect something specific. Sidhe contact is not a serious, heavy event with grave consequences and obligations. It is a getting acquainted process with a seemingly new neighbor. How might this be? Nobody can tell. After

all, there are innumerable ways of meeting new folks in our life. The only difference here lies in the fact that the neighbors are not entirely human, but closely related at the same time. Be open and have interest in exchanging kindness, even if you do not seem to register specific details. This part of the process might be full of surprises. The first time I sensed Fjeldur it was a noticeable presence with atmosphere and intention, and gradually I learnt to distinguish it as I can differentiate between how it feels to meet different people around me.

Sidhe contact is not an ascetic or austere business. It is as diverse as human contact. If you reach out on the wavelength of a gentle and friendly heart and an invitation to good neighborship, you will receive an equivalent response. Something wonderful, meaningful and joyful will likely unfold and it might be the beginning of a completely new journey.

Meeting Our Relatives

It is in this spirit that I share glimpses from trusted friends and colleagues who have agreed to share deeply personal experiences. I thank them for their willingness, and I hope the following journey will encourage you to make your own investigations. There is no claim-making in the following words. Instead they can be considered as footnotes and diary-extracts from the field of personal experiences. From the many friends I have in the large network of Lorian Association and the work of David Spangler and others, I have been enriched by many sharings from experienced people around the world. I am happy also to add a Nordic contribution to the growing fellowship of Sidhe-engaged people with gentle hearts and bright minds.

I want to emphasize that it is a great privilege to be able to share a variety of personal experiences from a diverse group of people who are consciously living with the Sidhe dimension in their personal lives. Considering how swift and natural these openings to the Sidhe realm have unfolded, and how deeply the inner recognitions have been, it is a great surprise that so much valuable insight and connection

U/ for u
I have many questions

has been mostly suppressed and unconscious in earlier life. From the very first workshops I facilitated on my own, and through the many succeeding weekends Sussie, my life-partner, and I have had together with so many amazing people, both from Scandinavia and perhaps a dozen other countries, it has been awe-inspiring to help unlock so much authentic and meaningful qualities and subtle contacts. This is just a selection of encounters. Many more could be added.

When the Stone Barrow Opened

Jes Romme is a Danish Natureguide, a teacher in Biology and a spiritual teacher as well. For decades he has worked with nature and animal communication and he is skilled in teaching about the way birds, animals, insects, trees and flowers live and survive in nature. I have known Jes for years and he has an impressive insight into nature, a deep appreciation for natural phenomena and for understanding how the biology and anatomy works. He is a trained observer with a sense of detail and beauty. He always leaves me with a sense of deep appreciation for his ability to observe, describe and care for nature. He is not the typical person one would suspect to have Sidhe contact, but for Jes it is effortlessly natural, and he doesn't mind sharing his experiences. To him they are simply an extension of the visible ecology of the natural world, and he understands the Sidhe are different from devas and nature spirits. Here he describes an important contact during a weekend workshop I held some years back:

"I am together with Søren and a group of people at Mols in Jutland, Denmark, where we visit the Poskær Stenhus, the largest stone barrow in Denmark, more than 5,000-years-old and with 23 standing stones. When I ask for permission to enter the inner field of the place, immediately I feel welcomed. I enter quietly in the gap where the missing 24th stone once was. Inside I am met by a subtle, light energy. I walk around inside the stone circle and notice the different forms and patterns of the stones as I sense them. Suddenly I see the stone I simply have to lean against in sitting position. Here, with the open space in front of me, and the stone chamber at a distance, I lean back and sense the form of the stone against my back.

"I close my eyes and sense the hardness of the standing stone. I lean my head against the stone. Being relaxed I soon open myself to a quiet atmosphere filled with inner presence. Something in me changes. I feel the hard structure of the stone against my back transform into a lively softness and support—and I melt into it. After some time, to my inner sight I become aware that the surface of the earth in front of me, in the central area of the stone circle, starts to grow into a big pile. It is clear that something from below is pressing upwards and it comes in push after push like a molehill being formed. I let go of my speculations about what it might be, and simply observe. Suddenly the molehill bursts open, and a long, zigzag-formed crack appear and grows, widening up towards me.

"Something moves in the huge crack, wanting to come up. And up comes humanoid personalities in full human size. Despite this they are different from us. First appear two horses with riders. Several people walk beside the horses. Several more appear through the big crack in the earth and they all align on both sides of the horses and look at me. Behind them several more keep coming up in a continued flow and position themselves in rows behind the first. At last the movement stops, but I see that many more move inside the crack and below the surface of the earth. It is a large crowd. The atmosphere is trustful, colored by melancholy, but also with a touch of solemnity. There is a calmness in the crowd. They observe me. With their massive and overwhelming presence, I sense they want something from me. Nothing is communicated to me directly. However, I experience support from them to my journey in life. I am filled with gratitude that they exist and for what I sense they do by their presence in this moment. Although I am in a condition of timelessness, I experience that the scenery seems to take quite some time. At last the crowd fades away and they are gone. I open my eyes, filled with a light and joyful mood. Our

Poskær Stenhus
Stone Barrow at Mols Bjerge in Jutland, Denmark

group is still within the stone circle, each of us sitting at a stone. Shortly after Søren let us know that we can rise and gather in the center of the stone circle.

"This experience is unique in my life. It is also my first experience with the Sidhe. The incident was so surprising and intense that I forgot to look closer at their facial features and how they were dressed. However, there was a nobleness around them. The form of their faces was oval, the expression melancholic and with no special mimic. I have repeatedly contacted these Elves when I needed a specific help in healing and animal communication. From the crowd one individual would then stand forth and give support, being a female or a male. Each time I have sensed this specific touch of seriousness around them."

With Bluish Skin and Heads Shaped Like a Star

The Sidhe can appear in ways we do not expect and emanate a presence and look that seems to be very exotic to our habitual perception. Their colors and appearance often seem to provoke our conventional views, but they also seem to be very natural. After all, we humans can also change our exterior form through fashion, culture and nationality. The Sidhe can also assist us in surprising ways and simply offer help or healing.

Carolina was a member of the Findhorn Foundation, with a background in Marketing and Human Resources. She worked partly as an organizer and a participant on a three-day Sidhe-workshop I had with Sussie at Findhorn in October 2019. One of our sessions took us out into nature under the pine trees close to the sea. Carolina had received a phrase during an exercise, saying: "*Trust your Impressions. Do not add, do not subtract.*" Reflecting on this, she had an unexpected encounter:

"As part of Søren and Sussie's workshop, we immersed ourselves as a group into the Hinterland at the Findhorn Community. While walking into the forest of pine and birch trees, with lots of green shiny moss on the ground, five or six Sidhe joined us from the left flank. They were tall, muscular, with bluish skin and heads shaped like a star, with no hair. They walked tall, with purpose, in their full power and sovereignty. While walking deeper into the trees, a male Sidhe held my left hand and elbow, and a female did the same with the right, guiding me to touch a particular pine tree. They then proceeded to touch my lower back, each with one hand, exactly where I was experiencing pain. It felt as if they were communicating with a sense of "we know the pain that you feel, and we are healing you."

Unexpected Contacts and Rainbows in the Heart

Alice Weibull is a Swedish clinical psychologist and healer. She has an extensive background with the Findhorn Community since the early 1970s. She attended our Sidhe Guide School in Denmark and after a while shared with us that she had experienced contact for years:

"Since I was young, I have had contact with angels and nature spirits, and therefore I was not surprised when I experienced contact with the Sidhe people at the first Sidhe-workshop. It was a green man with a feather in his hat, somewhat like Snufkin in the Moomin series by Tove Jansson. The first time he was simply standing in a valley full of flowers and grass. He felt somewhat hesitant, or perhaps I was. The next day we met again when Søren guided a morning meditation. I only heard a fragment of what Søren said as I was invited into the world of the green man. It was a short visit during the meditation. However, a dialogue had begun. During the year after the experience I have had several, similar contacts with the Sidhe world. It has occurred under different circumstances, in different places and ways. Here I will share a little bit about these meetings.

"The next contact with the Sidhe world happened as I was traveling to another workshop and found myself on the railway station in Gothenburg in Sweden. I took the opportunity to visit The Garden Society close to the railway station. I sat down by a small wall by a hill, a delightful place I felt drawn to. I tuned into the hill and there I met 'the blue man.' It is someone I have known for many years and he has been present during several healing sessions as my invisible helper. During this meeting I realized that the green man with the feathered hat and the blue man was in fact the same individual. He could simply shapeshift.

"Suddenly I was lying in a field inside a huge cave, the size of a big ballroom. My Sidhe friend—and I knew him as a friend—was next to me and we were stargazing. I felt baffled, and things started to fall into place. Later I understood why I had experienced such recognition and deep resonance when I first heard about the Sidhe people. During another workshop with Søren and Sussie the name Irloi came to me and since then this is what I have called my Sidhe friend. For me, live music is a strong opening to contact. I experienced this for the first time when my daughter and son-in-law invited me to the Concert House in Gothenburg.

During this tribute concert to Kate Bush I closed my eyes, let the music fill my body, as if my skin was breathing in the notes. Suddenly a landscape opened to my inner sight and I danced into it with Irloi. We danced together with others, like moving waves. The trees also danced, together with the brown leaves. After dancing between the trees, we entered a great hall with white columns. Here dancing continued right up to the roof. I felt a deep happiness.

"During another concert I closed my eyes during a song about longing. Suddenly I was standing with Irloi and a blue web embraced us as if we were closely enfolded. I asked sincerely what I have to give to the Sidhe world. The answer came in rays full of all the rainbow colors from my heart all around my body. Shortly after a guest singer appeared on stage singing 'I have rainbows in my heart.'

"During an Earth Healing workshop with Marko Pogacnik in Finland I got my first contact with Solara. She was yellow, warm and with a light energy, emanating much joy and invited me into her world. During my latest visit at Findhorn I got in contact with a Scottish Sidhe man with the name Farlei. I met him during a walk in the forest at Cluny Hill. Since then I have discovered that they know each other and from time to time they come to me as a group.

"Contact with the Sidhe requires complete awareness and openness in my whole body. If I lose my focus they disappear. I experience it as if I need to 'open my body' as it is possible to do in complete awareness with music, in nature or under the stars. This is my way of contacting. From time to time I forget all about my Sidhe friends. For example, at the turn of the year I was occupied with moving to another place, and they let me know that they would still be there when I was ready. To me there seems to be endless discoveries in contacting the Sidhe world. The more of us who open the doors within, the easier it will become to travel and exchange between the human and Sidhe world."

Sangvia in the Air

Annegrete Bugtrup is an accomplished psychotherapist with her own practice at Præstø in Denmark. I have known her for years, and I have had the honor of educating her in the SoulFlow Method and to have her attending many of my workshops, including the Sidhe Guide School, Sussie and I have together. Annegrete can enter the *real* world of imagination with an intensity and liveliness I have rarely come across. The very fact that she is a married mother with a demanding work as teacher and psychotherapist gives a solid foundation for her inner, wild openness, that has created a poetic contact to a female Sidhe. Annegrete loves poetry herself and has written many really beautiful poems in Danish. Once when I visited Annegrete we took a walk in the beautiful nature around her home, and a female Sidhe approached us and commented on our exchanges in her own, delightful ways. We attract what resonates with us. This goes for relations in the outer world as well as in the inner realms. Knowing Annegrete it makes a lot of sense why she is connecting with an individual like Sangvia—so vivid, so intense, yet with mildness. Here Annegrete shares in her own words how it all started:

"Meeting Sangvia started spontaneously and changed my life radically. Two years after our initial contact I realized that she was a Sidhe. During the two years I was full of longing, and from time to time I felt almost sick of longing. Her figure, her hair, her wild energy, gauzy and yet rooted, gentle and demanding, sensual and dancing. Who was she? Would I ever meet her again, and why did I react so powerfully when she appeared? Finally, she was there, and now with a name. Sangvia. SangviaaaaaaaaaaaaaaaAAAAHHHHH it came out of the blue air. I love that name. It sings and dances—soundtracks in eternal change. Sangvia is an insisting nature. She wants SO much in the connection with me. She comes when I call her, and yet she is already there. She changes her form as I change my thoughts. She changes element with the same ease as I blink to keep my eyeballs moist. I have recorded a lot about her that I want to write here, but she insists to be "live" and to communicate directly with me. The following is a communication with her in images. The words are my interpretation.

"'I walk around in your home. Investigate. Research. See how you stand by the sink and look out of the window, across the waters and at the pine trees where I reside, from time to time. I giggle, and I see how you sit in the sofa in the evening, looking at television, holding your husband in your hand. I look at your bed. A big, white square—soft. Unknown territory. Now I have to move on.'

"Sangvia becomes a spiral that transforms into a gigantic snail shell. The spiraling snail shell makes figure-of-eight movements in the air, connects my home with her preferred place outside 500 meters from my home. She is so active now, so I ask her what she thinks I should write. This is what she gives me through images and words:

"'You should come, all of you. Be with me in nature. You should look deep into the sea, gaze deep into the Earth—much deeper than you normally do. You think you see it all, but you don't. There are so many layers. We should take each other's hands—be united in this. It is much deeper than you think, much higher than you dream about.'"

The Green Friend

Eva Søborg Larsen works as a senior pedagogue in a forest Kindergarten near Elsinore in Denmark. She is also educated as a psychotherapist and SoulFlow Guide and has attended numerous Sidhe workshops and the Sidhe Guide School. I have known Eva for many years and cherish her flowering, humorous and healthy approach to life with a firmly rooted practicality and a widely open spirituality. Working in her forest Kindergarten Eva connects not only with the children she loves, but also with an inner awareness of the presence where they are. Here is her sharing about the green friend that has become part of her world:

"He danced forth on my left side, light, playful, merry, fanciful and with lots of whimsy, creativity and imagination. I was struck by his gentleness and his presence became more and more recognizable to me, the more I allowed it. He came out of a peaceful mound in the forest behind me—leaping out of the green blanket I leaned against numerous times.

"He was and became my support and inspiration in the many gatherings with the children outside in my Forest Kindergarten. He was tending the fire, so to speak. The fire burning in me, in nature, in the clown and the comics coming alive during the sessions we had. His energy weaved into mine, into the magical field I created at this very place together with the children—in storytelling, in sharing and in making inventive games. We were sucked into a world of play, dance, voices and magic and I was inspired deeply in ways I didn't understand, by something that just kept flowing through me and created an optimal space of excitement, wonder and laughter.

"I first felt his presence long after he invited himself into my small circle of children and life. Perhaps he was attracted to the energy and the living vibrations dancing here day after day—year after year. Perhaps he popped out with the beech tree at spring, who knows? However, one day our energy gathered there over the fireplace and the magic expanded significantly. A flow rushed through me and the hair stood up on the back of my neck as I rejoiced. I felt I had a new dancing partner, a helper, a green friend who backed me up.

"I became free, more alive, more dancing. I was flying without losing my sense of grounding. There was a strong power like green roots making me stand firmly in the life and wildness that blew through the field. There was joy and upliftment and the children loved it, loved the wild wind that opened their hearts—even the shy girl and the cautious boy opened and set themselves free. The other adults also joined and embraced the wings of magic and we soared together in a wholeness where we could support, contribute and give each other input of rare quality. After such gatherings we were high and when our green friend silently withdrew to the forest again, I am sure he also returned enriched with experiences and a gentle laughter in his heart.

"So, the fireplace in my small Kindergarten is the fountain of magic. It is the source of making the Elvenforce alive. Here bubbles the magic and poetry, the dance, the song and the shapeshifting in the huge, black cauldron of imagination, surrounded by trees with whispering leaves. Here small children and gentle adults can live and express their Elvenforce and joy. Here lives the real elvenfire, the wild dragon, the soft wind and the firm grip in the living door handle of the Earth. Here we can be ourselves. We can laugh, play, mold and live as the creatures we truly are in a beautiful green dance with our fellow creatures."

Portal Connections

Ron is a Lorian member who I have known for years. He has specialized in co-creating portals in wood in a beautiful and very special connection with the Sidhe. Ron is a woodworker, business consultant, and former entrepreneur. He is a lifelong spiritual explorer having participated in groups established by students of G.I. Gurdjieff, then studying core shamanic practices. For the past two decades he has worked with Incarnational Spirituality, becoming a Lorian priest and a member of the Lorian Board. His love of woodworking and nature brought him into contact with the Sidhe some years ago and he has nurtured that connection ever since. His commitment to working with the Sidhe has brought him new perspectives of our human engagement with Gaia which he is sharing through his woodwork and the Portals Connect website. In his own words:

"My connection with the Sidhe began about nine years ago. I sensed a tentative, subtle nudge to my shoulder from something while sitting on a sand dune at the seashore. For some inexplicable reason I began to think about the Sidhe. My only source of knowledge about them at the time came from John Matthews' book, *The Sidhe, Wisdom from the Celtic Otherworld*. After that first touch I occasionally sensed someone was looking over my shoulder. Was it my imagination?

"As these brief contacts continued, I accepted them as genuine. I was drawn to explore further. Simultaneously, David Spangler and Jeremy Berg were publishing the *Card Deck of the Sidhe*. Inspired by the Sidhe, this card deck intentionally creates a gateway to their world. Over some period of time, I worked with the Gate images until I could sense the energies that each card embodied.

"The cards create a subtle bridge between the Human and Sidhe realms. The layout is in the form of a cross. The vertical arm rising from the earth to the stars. The horizontal arm crossing from dawn to twilight, expressing the energies of the radiant sun and the reflective moon. By invoking the energies inherent in these card images, I have, after much practice over a number of years, been able to create and sustain a short, strong connection with the Sidhe.

"My substantial collaboration with the Sidhe began with the idea of making wooden portals; and concurrently the words, Elven Gates, popped into my mind. This work continued over several years. Initially, the Sidhe inspired the design of the portals. As I continued my work with them, our collaborative relationship grew. I discovered that I could discuss specific questions about the energetic flow through the form and substance of the portal. I would describe a fabrication challenge. Did they have any ideas? They often responded that they would consider it and reply later. These 'replies' were bursts of energy resolving themselves in creative visualizations. They evoked a solution, I divined its form."

**One of the Sidhe-portals Ron made,
with the Sidhe Glyph at its center**

"Over time I sensed a connection with specific Sidhe individuals. Three people began to resolve. They were a couple with a young daughter. We began to meet each other on a regular basis. I was intensely curious about their realm. How did they live? Did they have homes? Did they eat and have meals? They were quite willing to share with me. But my innate apprehension of our world, as a physical being, does not easily translate into an understanding of the subtle Sidhe realm. Once their daughter showed me a fast flowing 'creek' but I only discerned a 'gray' flowing 'something.' I could not see all the bubbling cascades of energy that made up its flow.

"What we do share as a common understanding is an emotional language. We love and honor one another. We appreciate each other's caring for others. We respect the work that each of us is doing to build bridges between Human and Sidhe. This couple and their daughter are more than friends, they are family. And as a family we are working together with the resources that we each have to enable more Humans and Sidhe to connect. As one of the Sidhe I met impressed upon me: 'We are one People.'"

"You Are Already There"

Christel Schneidermann is a Sound and Bodyhealer and also a Spiritual teacher who has specialized in facilitating meditations in nature. Her gentle being and natural connection to nature is something that defines her to a great extent, and it is a joy to be part of her world. Her response to the Sidhe teaching is one of the most instant and natural I have experienced, and I am absolutely sure she is attuned to the Sidhe field in a way so natural, that it is sometimes difficult for her to explain. In her own words:

"My contact with non-physical beings is not something I have consciously sought out. For many years they have come to me in a natural, meditative space. When I meditate, I experience that my field expands—and here, meeting subtle beings can occur. Spontaneous contacts often happen when I meditate in nature. They have been strong and deeply touching encounters, but I have not felt a need to find words or categories for my inner meetings. However, it caught my interest when I heard about Søren's teaching about the Sidhe people. It awakened a deeper interest and curiosity within me. I work as a teacher in meditation and personal development and for a while I had been searching for new inspiration. In February 2018 I received a mail from Søren about a Sidhe Guide School he and Sussie offered to people. My whole body quivered, and my heart was pounding, and I did not hesitate for a second to attend the school. Within an hour I registered. My heart rejoiced. It was a feeling that this was something I had been waiting for.

"One night before the start of the school I sensed an inner contact and the name Isildur arose in my consciousness (and yes, I know the name is also used by Tolkien, but this was what I heard). It became a very strong contact to a female, creative Sidhe, even before the start of the school. There is a deep feeling of love and connectedness when I sense her as an old friend I have missed, and who has appeared again. It feels like something I recognize and know while the Sidhe-field is also new to me, at least consciously.

"Isildur confirms much of the work I do, and honors me, and I feel deeply touched every time I sense it. During one of the first meetings she said: 'You are already there,' meaning that what I do was already a portal to the Sidhe. Especially she referred to my creative use of sound and painting.

"Meeting the Sidhe gave me the courage to forge a new path in my teaching and I realized that I had to terminate a job I had for several years. I needed to give more access to teach groups outside in nature. I should start becoming a living bridge between their world and ours. I also experienced that a clearing and cleansing of relations and things in my life had to be started. It was as if I pressed a button that accelerated inner and outer processes. I am certain that it is my contact to the Sidhe people that has been the catalyzer and inner support. I am deeply grateful, honored and humble to have been given these experiences and I am looking forward to explore, learn and play with our Sidhe brothers and sisters in a continued journey of discovery."

At the Iconic, Irish Faery Fort

Mary Reddy is a visual artist, writer, and Lorian priest living in the US. She participated in a Sidhe-journey I held with many people in North West Ireland in the autumn of 2019, and during our visit to the famous Ben Bulben in the Sligo area, known for its many Sidhe stories and often called a Faery Fort, she had a beautiful encounter:

"Communication with the Sidhe takes place telepathically for me, flowing in images and emotions. What I remember afterward often feels like less than actually took place. In connecting with the Sidhe on the slopes of Ben Bulben in Sligo, I felt myself sink into the mountain where a number of Sidhe greeted me. I sensed I was inside a dwelling with tall elegant cathedral-like arches. I had an impression of lovely colors and light. I began to describe to the Sidhe what it's

Ben Bulben
The huge Faery Fort in county Sligo, Ireland

like to be human on our side, so immersed are we in matter. I wanted them to know us better. I conveyed in images how difficult our lives can be, how hard I've worked during my life to rise out of trauma and pain, and how precious to me are the strengths, insights, and compassionate love that have emerged from this struggle.

"I handed them a rolled-up sheaf of parchment papers and told them 'These are maps of the human hearts of all of us who have come to visit you today.' In return, they asked me to hold my hands out. They placed in my right hand a golden apple and in the left, a silver apple. I recognized these from a Yeats poem, *The Song of Wandering Aengus*, where an old man seeks out his youthful vision of a 'glimmering girl' and imagines walking with her in long dappled grass, plucking '… till time and times are done, the silver apples of the moon, the golden apples of the sun.'

"Then I left the grassy slope, drawn by the musical sound of water below, weaving and splashing its way around curving banks and great midstream rocks. Over a bridge, then carefully across boggy ground, I came to the edge of the stream, took off my hiking boots and thick socks and plunged my feet into the cold water. The

Sidhe and I resumed our conversation. I watched them working closely with the spirits of the water, the rocks, and plants. After enjoying the activity for some time, I asked them 'What is your concern here? What is your science?' In response, they showed me a fish that looked like a large salmon. It rose halfway out of the water, its mouth gaping open. I was shocked to realize it was dead. As my rational mind began to race over thoughts of poisoned waters and species extinction, the Sidhe pulled me back. They immediately flooded my being with joy, the utter beauty of the water dancing over the rocks, the richness of the different shades of green across the land, the brightness of the blue sky and white clouds, the wind drying my wet feet. My worries ceased, my heart lifted.

"Meetings with the Sidhe always contain a mystery. This one felt important to me—that they returned me to joy, that they abide in joy."

"Our Contact Is Non-Verbal"

Annette Pomiklo works as a Senior Project Officer in a small business company. She has a background as translator and her work as project officer in the world of natural sciences goes well with her academic brain. Despite many educations and workshops within the spiritual and holistic world, she was not—in her conscious mind—prepared to work with the Sidhe, in herself and around her. Somehow it seemed to be too strange! Nonetheless, her heart would not stay quiet and she surrendered to the inner call. Personally, I have found Annette to be so much attuned to the Sidhe dimension that her hesitation almost seems to be funny. Annette has a deep resonance with the Sidhe, and it is definitely not limited to her brain capacity or her brilliant mind. She is what one could call "a natural." Yet, again it is a reminder that we are so much more than conventions and mainstream culture. For Annette, the Sidhe realm has enhanced ethical dimensions as well as her ability to write stories. She reveals that beside her inner awakening there is something more:

"I have a female contact in the Sidhe realm. We don't meet often. I do not conjure her. Suddenly she can be present under the light green leaves of the beech tree, or when my light green crystal heart, given by her, is awakened during a sound massage. Our contact is non-verbal. Her language is the lightness and beauty and, in this field or atmosphere we meet. Her name is like a rippling brook or ringing crystals. I also have another contact, a wild woman or a female shaman living within a mountain."

Time for Merging

Sheena Mariah Nielsen is educated as a Rudolf Steiner pedagogue. She is a healer, facilitator and co-leader of The Golden Circle in Denmark where she lives with her daughter. I admire her for her wholehearted dedication and her determination to bring renewal in healthy and balanced ways where she has placed her commitment. Sheena Mariah has resonated clearly to the call of the Sidhe and she has been a valued participant on our Sidhe Guide school. She has a vision to integrate the Sidhe dimension into the place where she lives.

"I have been calling the Sidhe people and asked if they wanted to cooperate. They already knew that I came as they are closely connected via telepathy and I have contact with a Sidhe woman who follows me. I sit on one of the dragon mountains—a burial mound with feminine energies close to where I live. I have often contacted the Sidhe during wintertime and in the early spring where I experienced them sitting inside the Earth-Mounds in a ceremony about the waters of life, the light, the year cycle, the flowering and more. They have always been beautiful and tender meetings, awakening a deep resonance within me. Often the meeting ends with an exercise, a gift or some words that can support me on my journey. Now it is Midsummer, and I have not had Sidhe contact for a long time.

"I hear these words from a male Sidhe: 'We are everywhere, outside and inside, but not restricted by the physical form like

Humanity. We are behind all life and in everlasting movement, always intimately connected with The Mother, the seasons on Earth and the Source we originate from. We are very varied, and we have very diverse responsibilities. What you see depends on who you are and what purpose the meeting has. We experience that Humanity perceive separation everywhere—separation from nature, from each other, between the genders, and between us and you. Time has come for merging, for uniting in sacred ways—everywhere. Some of you are more awake and conscious about this, and we ask you to share your knowledge, share your experiences and share with each other.'

"The male Sidhe tells me that he participated when we created a beautiful nature-mandala at The Golden Circle a month earlier. I had invited all the Sidhe who live in the Mounds nearby and they came back to the center and participated in a beautiful mandala-ceremony. We wanted to create a nature-mandala of the gifts from nature— flowers, leaves, cones, feathers, sticks, crystals and stones—as a symbol of an opening into cooperation and friendship with the Sidhe and the devas. It was a really wonderful and heartfelt experience and I saw how the Sidhe circled around us and shared the joy of the dedication to cooperation. They thanked us for every little step we take towards cooperation and they rejoice over our conscious awareness in this."

A Rich and Diverse People

Elisabeth Dyrmose is a Sound Healer, Flute Player and Drummer who works in the universal shamanic lineage in her own way. She is also active in Grandmothers' Circle in Denmark and she has attended many of my Sidhe workshops and our Sidhe Guide School. Elisabeth has a wonderful approach to spirituality and has her unique song, coming from places where everything is still primordial and full of spring, joy and hope. I have cooperated with her several times and deeply appreciate her soul-path that resonates with the Sidhe wisdom. Elisabeth does not have dialogues with the Sidhe, but she has contact with them, as you will see in the following. She senses their presence as they connect with her, and she has experienced them in many varieties. Here comes an encounter with a male Sidhe:

"One day, when I gave a person sound-healing, who was lying on a couch beneath a blanket, I positioned myself at the person's feet and started drumming. While I was standing there, the Sidhe I call The Priest, came and put his Sidhe-mantle of opal-shining invisibility over the client. He stood there for a while and then disappeared from my sight. It was incredibly beautiful, and I was moved by it. I met The Priest for the first time during an inner journey where he was standing in a glass castle welcoming me in a magical world of weird creatures, life forms and a deep, dark blue lake that was transparent and clear.

"Occasionally he comes when I sing or express myself in natural healing song. During these visits I sense his wish that we Humans need to get started. I sense his intense impatience over our slow pace when it comes to act bravely for the Earth and all its inhabitants and their wellbeing. He almost pushes me in the back if he wants me to communicate something to one or more persons. I often experience it is as if it is him speaking through me, especially when I speak in a way I do not know, and yet recognize. Some people call it star language. I call it elven language. When the speech comes, I am in elven land in the realm of Tolkien. I sense the listeners are touched and melt because of it. As an ancient memory being activated, from before sounds and words as we know it, in a longing so old, that it is almost forgotten."

The Chief and Lady Glenfire

On many occasions Sussie told me about Øm Jættestue, a beautiful and impressive passage tomb or megalithic mound not far from Lejre in Denmark. It is clad in grass and surrounded by a small, green area with trees. This place has a special significance to her, and she has felt drawn to it on special occasions.

In the time leading up to her first contact with me she felt encouraged to go there. For a period, she went out there several times during a week and she was deeply touched. She realized that she was in contact with living, non-physical presences and she clearly felt that it did not relate to angels.

From time to time a distinct presence came forth. She felt a peculiar form of sensuousness and a feeling that there was a male presence very closely related to her own human nature. There was a sense of relatedness. It moved her deeply and she was certain that this was not an angelic being. She sensed it as a male presence with a posture like a chief. He has a dignified presence, a nobleness radiates from him, and he is both an individual and nature becoming alive. In the contact she realized that she had been met in a way so she could not feel lonely in the same way anymore. She was encountering a presence with a psychology not far from her own and yet different. She was mirrored or reflected by this presence she could not see with her physical eyes, and yet perceived with clarity and depth. The male presence that perceived her in wholeness, reminded her of her own human nature in a new way. She returned to the place many times and the intimacy deepened as she realized it was an encounter displaying the features of the Sidhe.

At other times there has been an entirely different, female presence with bright, flaming red hair, emerald green, bright eyes, very sharp facial features, full lips, high cheekbones, pointed ears and a surprising gentleness, considering the unusual, noticeable face. She is dressed in white and is in company with two young presences she seems to care for like a mother. This female Sidhe has communicated to Sussie that her name has a meaning that corresponds to the word *Glenfire*. She is a distinct personality resembling a human being to a certain extent. Until now there has not been a specific agenda, so the encounters have mostly been mutually interested observations. Sussie has no sense of what this encounter with lady Glenfire is about. Perhaps it is the slow beginning of a future relation. Perhaps it is simply a cordial hello from a distant relative. Time will show.

Sidhe Presence through Touch Drawing

Deborah Koff-Chapin is one of my American friends who I have met several times during events in the USA and Scotland. She is an internationally known artist and educator. Since originating the Touch Drawing process in 1974, she has introduced it at conferences and graduate programs internationally. Her SoulCards 1&2 are sold worldwide, and she is author of *Drawing Out Your Soul*.

Deborah has pioneered the function of Interpretive Artist at public events since 1982. Through the immediacy of Touch Drawing, she visually portrays the content and energetic qualities of a lecture, ceremony, or performance. She creates 6-8 drawings per hour that are displayed for the audience to reflect upon. Deborah has drawn during the presentations of over 800 different cultural and religious figures including the Dalai Lama, Archbishop Desmond Tutu, and all the plenary presenters of the 2015 Parliament of World Religions.

I am deeply impressed by her ability to tune in to subtle presences and engage in an instant, creative flow of expressing their atmosphere. During the Co-Creative Spirituality conference at Findhorn in 2018, where the Sidhe was one of the core themes for the first time at such an event, she was working in an ongoing, almost nonstop creativity during lectures and workshops, sharing her impressions of the beings emerging as inner partners of the event. She engages while listening to what is shared, and immediately the inner presences present themselves to her in the moment. As she has told me:

> "It is a simple yet profound way of making images through the touch of fingertips on paper that lays on a smooth surface of wet paint. Lift the page to see the impressions on the underside created by your touch. As I have practiced over the years, Touch Drawing has become a way to attune to subtle presence and bring it into form. I do not actually 'see' anything before drawing. Rather, I feel sensations and translate them into images on the page. When I draw a face, it is as if a being is taking shape beneath my fingertips.

I often wonder about these faces—does a subtle being really need a nose? My understanding is that the human face is a language we most naturally relate to. A being can make itself available to me as a translator of its presence into human form."

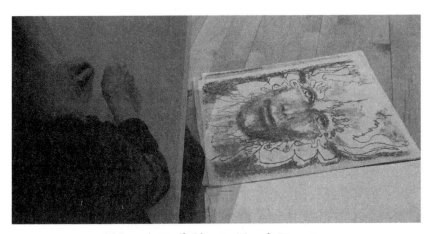

Deborah Koff-Chapin Touch Drawing

Touch Drawing of Sidhe Presence by Deborah Koff-Chapin

This is a beautiful and unique example of how the creative flow can open living portals between the worlds, and in Deborah's work it is done through the special method of Touch Drawing. You can see much of it on her website shared in the back of this book. On the previous page you see a Sidhe that was drawn during a talk by Jeremy Berg at the Findhorn conference in 2018, and below is a Sidhe presence during my presentation at the Gaianeering Conference at Bastyr University in Kenmore Washington, the year before.

A Faun Emerges

Earlier I touched briefly on the nature of what I call The Kingdom of Pan or The Children of Gaia. Here is an example on how it can be a learning process to discover the differences between these beings and the Sidhe. Sussie and I led a Sidhe workshop at a Danish Highschool in May 2019. During a meditative attunement with music Sussie detected a presence on her left side. She had her physical eyes closed, but with her inner attention she turned her focus to the left to look closer and she discovered a face. It was very peculiar, somewhat resembling a humanoid presence, and at the same time the profile of the face was slightly looking like a cat in the brow and nose area. On the cheeks and brow, she noticed spiral ornaments on the skin and there was a golden and green atmosphere. Sussie thought that this may be a Sidhe and she was fascinated by the ornaments.

She looked closer. The eyes were somewhat oblique, giving associations to an animal. She could see parts of the torso and it was a male—naked and muscular. Further below the figure was diffuse. She focused more closely at the face and discovered small, fluted spiral horns. In an instant it dawned upon her: *"Oh my God... they really LOOK like that!"* It became acutely clear that she was not imagining—she saw this, and it was absolutely real. Something seemed to fall into place. She was looking right into a world that was very much alive. She could sense the atmosphere. Sussie knew how important it is in Sidhe contacts to establish a relationship in deep connectedness. It did not happen here at all. She was looking at a Faun right next to her. He was listening to the music being played in the room. Something important had caught his attention. There was an essence in the music, a sound from his own world. The music to him was a kind of call, a call of recognition to him. In some way he is reminded of something important. An atmosphere of deep slowness was increasing, a continuation as if time was not there at all. Ancient—and at the same time beyond time. There was also an aloneness to him—not loneliness, but aloneness, and yet a sense of being completely embedded in nature—of being the root of nature.

Besides these peculiar features Sussie picked up another important thing. She was not in any way able to connect with the consciousness of the Faun. It was as if the frequency was empty. Yet, there was awareness, and the sense was that he was completely amoral. There seemed to be the absence of the kind of morality we humans know so well. It was very strange, yet also simply a recognition of the fact, that this is how it was. This creature did not owe anyone anything. It was completely entrenched in a state of no guilt, no shame, no awareness of right or wrong, no morality. It was just how it was. Natural. Primordial. Yet, it was present right there, close to Sussie, and it was just how it was. As the music piece ended, the Faun faded away.

The Sidhe Assembly at Grianan of Aileach

I would like to end this series of sharings by including an important experience I shared while facilitating an Irish Sidhe journey with Sussie and a large group of co-travelers in 2018. We were in the NW-part of Ireland at a hillfort in County Donegal. We were in the concluding phase of the week-long journey and we sat in heather, surrounded by a great view in nature. Three from our company had just been singing inspired songs and we sat with closed eyes and meditated. Suddenly I became aware that we were being greeted by a gathering of Sidhe. I hesitated but decided to say aloud what

I perceived. I felt like an interpreter and it was difficult as I was trying to convey something coming from "organic-mentality," but I only had the human "metal-language" to use. The gathering was in front of me, perhaps around ten Sidhe representatives, but perhaps several more I was unable to detect. They were very different from each other like a diversified bunch of people of many trades who had gathered because of a shared purpose. Most of them I sensed as silhouettes and one of them lighted up and reminded me of one of the Sidhe painted by AE. It was a male with a golden glow and a multicolored headdress. On behalf of all the gathered Sidhe there was a clear intention of trying to come across to my world and our circle, and the content was this:

"We are here, a gathering of Sidhe, greeting you. We are here to remind you of our manifold nature. We are very different from each other, just like you, and yet we are one people, one civilization with many clans and groups. We are amongst you, here and now, to let you know that we appreciate your journey and your attempts to build bridges between you and us. Remember our diversity so you do not end talking about us in a too simplified or naïve way. It is not easy to cross the abyss and let our people meet after so long a separation and we have developed very differently. At the same time, we are essentially one world. New beginnings are emerging, and we find each other in new attempts, just like you do. Because of this we are gathered here today to remind you of our multicolored and diverse worlds. We appreciate your interest and we bow in front of you as we greet you with warmth. Remember the diversity so the bridge between us can grow strong. Be greeted!"

I sensed the depth and clarity, but also the solemnity from the gathering, remarkably silent as they stood there. I sensed how much they were aware that it involves certain risks to exchange with us due to past misunderstandings and our tendency to idolize them and destroy good opportunities. I sensed amongst them representatives from many of the places we had visited, including the silvery glittering waterfall at Glencar, the wild, majestic and windswept cliffs of Horn Head and the beach and deep, moss-filled, green Hobbit-world of Marble Hills. The landscapes were present, woven into the presence of the representatives, and the golden speaker among them was a reminder of the lyrical paintings and poems of AE.

This sharing from personal encounters also is an appeal from me to encourage we humans to remain sober and sincere in our approach towards our Gaian relatives. We need to make the connection natural and not phenomenal. We need to avoid glamor and romances that end up derailing us from the importance and deeper values and opportunities we are being offered. There is so much to win and so incredibly much to lose in this renewed endeavor. Let us combine maturity and playfulness in beginning a new journey of shared awakening.

⊘ Gift ⊙
Open House Invitation

At any time, you can invite your "good neighbors." The Sidhe are very close to you, but if you consciously invite them to experience your human world, it becomes much easier for them to approach. Depth lies in simplicity. Sometimes we expect the deep stuff to be intricate and not within reach for newcomers. However, it is my experience that there is a great deceit in this attitude, and it is part of the game-changing discoveries to find out that the treasure is right where we stand.

Sidhe-contact is not for the few selected ones. In fact, we need to make things straightforward. Sidhe-contact is all about inviting your neighbors to a friendly meet. Plain and simple. No strange agendas or hyped anticipations. Simply a wish to connect with kindred spirits. The only thing you need is a clear invitation and hospitality. You may ask how this should be done with beings you cannot shake hands with? Well, act normal and do things knowing that all your guests need is an invitation. Again, you may ask, how? It is very simple.

Select a time and place. In your mind and with your heart, let your invisible guests know that they are wholeheartedly welcome to your place. You are the portal. You create an opening or a window through your invitation. Let the Sidhe know that you are interested in good neighborship and they are welcome in your life and home, especially at a certain time, like having open house. You are the host and they are invited to sense you and your world through you. Don't make it too serious. Don't make it complicated. Don't hype it and lose your sense of humor. After all, you are simply inviting guests for tea or coffee—symbolically speaking. Let the Sidhe know, that you are genuinely interested in showing them your life and home. They are welcome to see through your eyes and sense through your presence. You are not in any way inviting anybody to take over your body. It is not about channeling. It is not about letting go of yourself. On the contrary. Stay in your dignity and be yourself with kindness and interest. Let your Sidhe relatives feel welcome at the given time and let them sense how it is to be a human being. How it is to clean up, to make food, to tend flowers, to use your computer, to walk around and do things in your world. Show them things you care about. Improvise. Perhaps you want to sing a song for them. Perhaps you simply tell them things aloud. Or perhaps everything is done in silence. You can light a candle for them in a room and let them know that you appreciate good neighborship.

Don't expect anything special. Be present. Be yourself. Be kind and interested. You can be curious, and it is absolutely okay to notice and record things you observe. Perhaps you discover that you sense a response. Perhaps you are surprised to discover that someone is distinctly present. Perhaps you do not sense anything. Perhaps you register things later. The very act is a transforming thing as you signal something significant to them. In fact, any subtle being responding to your kind openness is welcome to pop in. However, your invite is specifically for the Sidhe.

Besides my own experiences I know of several people who have found this process to have a deep effect on them, and there is certainly an interest on the side of the Sidhe. After all, how often do they get an invitation like this? They pick up your intention and presence as you tune in on them. Rest assured. You are beaming out on their frequencies and they will be aware of your interest. From this a new relationship can grow—naturally and with mutual benefit.

No worries. This is not an encouragement to make spooky contacts. It is a very natural thing. The determining factor is intention with mind and heart. If you open with a sincere wish and remain being you, the response will come from similar frequencies. Equal attracts equal. If you find it relevant and it fits with your mentality, I warmly recommend that you make this open house invitation—not only once, but several times—and notice what new beginnings it can help emerge.

There are so many things to share about engaging with new contacts with the Sidhe, but this simple opening can be very powerful.

Part Two

The Wild Quest

It is time to turn your attention back to yourself.
Within you lie the keys to a new awakening.
It brings you back to the great Wildness.
It invites you to your forgotten Treasure,
The Hallows of the Lost Magic.
Are you ready?

3

THE GENTLE WILDNESS

Back into the Wild

Let us engage with the Sidhe in you and me. You and I—we are the untamed breath, deliberately captured and willingly embedded in an organic form of expression, called the body. You and I are the inextinguishable life, constantly propelling forward in a never-ending *YES* to manifest, show up and express. We are the inexhaustible expressions of the unnamable source behind all creation. Precisely and exactly. This is what we are. We are outrageously wild!

However—something happened along the way. It seems that we have almost lost our wildness. We have been tamed and we have tamed ourselves to a degree where we question the value of life and complain about the boredom of daily activities. Many people are in a constantly repeating loop of habitual daze, caught in the zombie-existence of superficiality. It is the same for rich and poor, whether you are wealthy or underprivileged—it simply manifests in different variations. Poverty might keep you on drugs and crime to survive, and wealth may lead you to drugs and crime to uphold your lifestyle. On a smaller scale, whether you are this or that, you are simply repeating the same routines every day, making them the content of your life instead of every day waking up to the wonders of being alive.

Being captured by norms and habits uphold a certain kind of comfort, but they also prevent you from feeling the deeper pulse in everything. You can stay in the safe-zone for a long time, but the price will be a growing dullness and a feeling that you are not arriving at the destined location—the train has left the station. This expands into a more and more unbearable feeling of being unfulfilled and unsatisfied, finally culminating in unhappiness. You simply can't stand observing the pale nature of your daily life and the world around you becomes a more and more scary place, full of threats and gloomy perspectives.

It may sound like a contradiction that we need to get back into the wild. We have used innumerable generations to evolve culturally, to sophisticate our living and gain relative independence from wild nature. We are proud of the inventions of advanced civilization, and it has given us many wonderful assets and convenient possibilities—at least in the economically prosperous parts of the world. However, it has also delivered some of the most challenging shadow aspects of so-called modern life. No need to list them. Just think about the alienation we have developed towards our natural surroundings, as if the natural world is an annoying obstacle to an urban life full of plastic flowers, grey concrete and sterile air-condition.

In a way we have imagined ourselves into small oxygen-deprived, artificial boxes, suffocating us while we complain about the primitive nature of our untamed surroundings full of the freshness of life. We have developed a blindness towards the obvious and a numbness towards the simple sensations of natural awareness.

We need to escape the strangling, self-imposed prisons of petty tininess and imagine ourselves back to the immenseness of existence—our very given and sacred birthright. We are on an escape mission. Spellbound by the alluring bling-bling of artificial confines and surrogate constructions, we must discover how to surf and avoid the restrictions of fake structures, and how to reconnect with the budding, branching greenness of reality. Our escape mission is all about rediscovering the freshness of the wind and the sweetness of a flower.

☉ Gift ☽
Do Something Aimless

Do yourself the favor of taking a little time to do something you normally don't do. It does not need to be spectacular at all. In fact, it can be a small thing that just takes five or ten minutes. If you can go outside and be in nature, do it now. If you cannot, stay inside and do it where you are. Let go of preconceived ideas and discover what happens when you are not focused on purpose or planning.

Outside

Give yourself permission to simply walk out without a specific idea about what to do. Perhaps you stumble over a stone or discover something you have never noticed before. You could perhaps find a tree or a flower. You could look very closely at its bark if it is a tree. Give your full attention to its structure. Does it look like something? Is there a melody inside the tree? What feelings does it awake in you when you touch it? Have you ever licked on bark, tasted it? Does the tree have a personality to you, an identity? What could you whisper to the tree? Look up and see the tree under the sky. Are you able to perceive or feel if it is slightly waving in the wind? How does it feel? What is the sound of its silence?

Inside

If you are in your home, why not go to a place where you have never really sat before and take your time to experience you and the place from a completely new angle. Is there a certain smell right where you are? Find an angle to look from, that is entirely new. What does it awake in you to sense it like that? Is there anything wild and untamed in the room, something that is not conformed or adapted by human hands? Does the room have a specific atmosphere? How would you describe it? Is there something around you that is neglected? If the room could speak, what would it say? Is it time for you to befriend something right where you are, and no matter what it is?

What you do is entirely up to you and it is crucial that you see it as an opportunity to break out of your shells of habitual behavior. A mainstream mindset could dismiss this whole thing as nonsense, but it is a genuine opportunity for you to create new space for a new awareness and you never attain this by repeating what you do already. If this suggested action therefore feels awkward to you, what else could you do that is seemingly pointless, aimless or random—yet sincere?

Untaming You

The journey back to wildness is the road to renewed sanity. However, be aware: You will become dangerous in the eyes of conformity and rigid norms, crystallized traditions and customs. Releasing you from the self-confined prison is not something that will be approved by widely accepted convention. You will be leaving the comfort-zone mentality and the highways of mainstream mindset. It is unsettling for many people who would rather have you stay in the well-trodden pathways of human behavior. It takes courage to awake to take the red pill and become unplugged.

Before going further, it is only natural to ask what it implies when you start releasing yourself and go rogue in the Sidhe-way. The answer is that no-one can tell you as nobody has been there before. Your path is in the making. Nevertheless, it is possible to share some general characteristics from experience.

Newness

You will enter an open landscape very different from the confining norms and repetitive habits you know so well. There will be an openness to the here and now, and it is completely unsentimental and free of reactions. Think for a moment how much repetitions frame ordinary life. A typical description of life will consist of daily routines and variations of well-known rituals and duties. Only from time to time certain rare surprises may turn up and usually they are gone in an instant and you are back in the humdrum of regular procedures. Waking up to the fresh newness of the moment is to start turning this around. It is as if the cracks in the walls of normality start to increase and expand and you face amazements and discoveries more often.

The Sidhe-nature in you and I breathes the air of constant renewal and is a foreigner to endless habitual repetition. Everyday life becomes tainted with a new unpredictability that may seem dangerous to many people, but which is welcomed by the awakening you. Daily life gradually starts to become extraordinarily ordinary. Things you did earlier with an almost zombie-like attitude reveals new layers. Looking at something starts having a freshness as if you have never really seen things like this before. Breathing in scents start stirring long forgotten yearnings in you. Meeting other people gives way to appreciating them in new ways you never thought of before.

Innocence

Innocence so often relates to being a child and the cynical mentality of so-called adulthood will inform you that growing up means to leave *"the naïve innocence"* and become a *real* person in the *real* world. This is not only extremely hurtful and callous, but also expresses disdain and resentment, stemming from disappointments and hurtful experiences. Innocence must be reclaimed amid a toxic world. Real adulthood in the wild sense is all about innocence and it is not naïve or childish. It relates to the open mind and heart we have from birth. Innocence resides within us and has never left us. Innocence is the most original part of us, and before it was wrapped in norms and conventions it was our natural skin, our way of connecting with the world.

Innocence carries with it a most delightful and appealing sensuality, uncorrupted by devious greed and possessive desire. It is a lusciousness of life itself, tingling with the gifts from all senses in the natural world. It is this aspect of our nature that lights up when we smile or give space to astonishment and pure curiosity. It brings us to places we never dreamt of and stimulates our creative genius.

Rejuvenation

Freeing yourself from the shackles of sleepiness empowers you with the resilience and optimism that should be the most obvious ABC of life. There is a rising force, a natural buoyancy, in the flow of life that defies the dominance of gravity. It is expressed as the "*Yes*" to endure and to manifest in the world, to leave new blueprints and steps never taken before. To befriend this upsurge of energy is to connect with the revitalizing flow that is available everywhere and at any time if we attune to it. From this well of plenty comes a sprouting and a branching in all directions. The vitalizing wave of life is everywhere in nature. Even when we humans lose our confidence in how to survive, our bodies continue to adapt and grow, reconfigure and shapeshift. Nature equals abundance. When we allow nature to connect with us through our senses, presence and awareness, we align ourselves with the restoring and youthful vigor.

Renewal always comes from the edge of things. It is potent where something ends and something else begins. Think of the energy in walking along the beach and feel how land and sea meet each other. Right there in the overlapping zone, where the waves lick the stones and the pebbles roll down into the wet element, there is much energy available. Rejuvenation is vitally pregnant in the membranes and the borderlines where exchange happens. So, you and I will need to visit the edges in our life in all sorts of variations. It is out there, on a limb, where we are surprised by things we never imagined and bestowed with energy and confirmation that there is so much in the becoming all the time. Rejuvenation is the tide of hope and trust, and you are part of it.

Let me exemplify how this is something that affects us in all our differences. There are so many examples of this extraordinary presence of newness, innocence and rejuvenation when people open themselves to the Sidhe field and start experiencing the inner stirring. Joan Kragh is a Danish Politician, Singer and Therapist. I have known her for years and it has been fascinating to be part of her journey into the Sidhe realm. It is also significant to know that the influence from her approach to the inner side of nature has been important for her political commitment to engage with society, culture and all our present human challenges, by joining the Danish Green Party, Alternativet. Joan is also educated as a singer and she has been trained in SoulFlow and participated in the Sidhe Guide School. For her, something incredibly important is stirring here and now:

"The wonder is everywhere in the new awakening. The experience of being in dialogue with stones, trees, animals, landscapes and the Sidhe has changed me radically. It has been a part of my wild journey back to my inner homeland. The language and the song have taken a different meaning and it cannot be staged. Dialogue appears when there is no distance between me and the others. I have met devas, stones, animals, landscapes and Sidhe and it has softened me. My wildness and inner poetry have been awakened. There is a greenness within me like never before. The sun in the heart heals my busy, daily life. It calls me to my inner homeland, but also to the outer quest, to adventures, new friendships and songs of light. Until now the journey has created song-lines from Denmark to The Pyrenees and back to Mols Bjerge National Park in Denmark, to the Faroe Islands, my true home that I love so strongly, and recently to Ireland in the west, where meeting the Sidhe, our shared mythology and future tasks converge. Together we will save our shared origin, Mother Earth."

I have had the privilege to be with Joan and many others and experience how it affects their being and doing. Belinda Bell has worked as an EHS Senior Consultant (Environmental, Health, and Safety Manager) and has a deep interest in how we take good care of nature and she is deeply engaged with organizational projects and leadership. She has been attending several Sidhe workshops and participated in the Sidhe Guide School. She emphasizes how much the Sidhe field created a deep, inner recognition and a great joy in her, when she met it. Part of it was new to her and other parts resonated consciously.

"Suddenly I got an understanding and deep respect for my own, strong connection to nature. It became clear to me that it was not just for silly fun and laziness that I can spend hours in nature and that I naturally find my way home when I am far away out there. It also made sense that I love the time in nature close to sunset and it is at this time I experience feeling safe and at home. Working with the Sidhe-field in workshops, I acquired tools to transform and harness the power and strength in the inner Sidhe-nature. This is a power and strength that is rooted in a primordial energy and feeling of connectedness with nature and its beings, a sense of companionship and care when I am in nature, and the possibility of taking it with me into other aspects of life.

"Understanding of how the connectedness to nature affects my life and the importance of it has made me aware of what happens in me when I am in the Sidhe-field, and today I bring it with me into other aspects of life. My close relationships, my professional contacts and my decisions are to some degree rooted in my inner Sidhe-nature. I experience myself more whole and authentic and I solve conflicts I encounter in my professional life in different ways than previously. I experience an ancient kinship awakening in me and supporting me, whispering to me in my ears when I am under pressure and need to find solutions. In the beginning it has felt a little strange, but I have improved my capacity to integrate these facets and to utilize the help I am given."

Rising out of the newness, innocence and rejuvenation is a deeply felt sense of dignity and ability to honor oneself. Annette Pomiklo experienced this:

"When I learnt about the inner Sidhe-nature, it opened to a new experience of myself and the world. It was easy for me to connect with the melancholy and dancing, playful lightness of the Sidhe realm, a paradox which is also very present in me and which I have struggled with for many, many years. Especially, the light facets have been revived and received more power. It is as if a greater balance between major and minor in me has been achieved, or perhaps just a greater flexibility of movements between the two, as if they were two sounds in the same song. I mirror myself in the natural dignity of the Sidhe people. Dignity has, especially, become one of the core values in my life, a value that has made it easier to be me, also in working relations. To me it is a beautiful value that gives a certain kind of calmness and anchoring."

The fixed and the flowing is the living duality around the eternal renewal, the peaceful innocence and the wonderful rejuvenating effect it has. Annette says:

"In the Sidhe-field I have met a free and playful version of closeness to nature and the natural forces, perfectly fitting with the one I am. I walk in nature with enhanced presence and always in deep, wordless communication with the elements and creatures I meet on the way. It is here I sense that I am connected, and it is here I can get inspiration to my stories. It is the combination of anchoring, nature-contact and poetry that attracts me when I connect with the Sidhe field. The fixed and the flowing. It plays well together. Add to this the mythical and mystical, the hidden, the beauty and the joy, the natural and the gentle, power and integrity. These are all elements I feel deeply connected with and that mirror themselves in me."

Jane Folsted is a friend and colleague with an extensive background in shamanism through three decades. She is an artist and educated as SoulFlow Guide, and she has attended our Sidhe Guide School. For many years she has been a Guardian for Moder Jords Have (The Garden of Mother Earth) in Northern Jutland in Denmark. Jane is a well-grounded, humble person with lots of humor and gentleness. She has experienced tremendous inspiration from engaging with the Sidhe field, and she works with imagination on her inner journeys and when she helps people:

"On my journeys between the layers and veils of the worlds, into the forgotten land where the Sidhe-power is present, everything is possible. This adventurous and magical landscape is a place where fabulous unfoldments emerge. Experience has taught me to lean into the scenery unfolding in my inner eye with full confidence and no drama. I take a leap of faith into the unknown and down into the darkness and I am reassured how the dark is cleansing, nurturing and lifegiving. After being washed in the depth I rise into the universal peace with a great view and many insights. These are journeys full of wonder and magic, giving strength and insight for my daily life in the outer reality."

Following these examples, ask yourself where you can feel something similar stirring within you. It is not belonging to never-never-land. It is right here and now.

◌ GIFT ◌
See the Wildness in a Face

Without staring uncomfortably at another person, make it a journey of discovery to look at other people's faces in a completely new way. Let us assert that you are lucky to be able to look at another person's face more than normally, without interfering or transgressing. If not possible, it could even be your own face seen in a mirror. Probably it is the easiest place to start.

Everything you look at is simply wild nature. The brow, the eyes, the chin, the lips and so on, are arranged in a completely unique way. No matter how much the person appears as a controlled, civilized and cultural citizen, the face is still wild architecture. We are creatures consisting of living materials that behave in fascinating ways. We are star-stuff materialized as organic beings. And we are light particles organized intelligently as intricate patterns.

Take a very fresh look as if you have never seen it before. Look carefully. You are looking into a world never experienced before.

Everything is living wildness. Everything is in constant change. Look at the unique pattern of the ear. Notice the curves of the nose. Experience the brightness and the unique inimitability of the eyes. See the hair. Take in the overwhelming world of the entire face as an enigmatic realm—quite simply an incredible universe in itself.

Sometimes the enigmatic unknown is, figuratively speaking, staring right at us, and we are completely blind to it, occupied with our surface scanning of repetitive recognitions. Distracted in our heads, absent minded and lost in speculations, we are removed from the stunning presence of the here and now, absorbed by memories of the past and images of the future. The revolution of awakening is the coming back to where we actually are, starting to wonder what on earth is going on. In this openness something new is stirring. Give yourself the gift of seeing wildness in a face— perhaps your own.

Your Life-Triskelion

Untaming you on your Sidhe-path is a way of activating your life-triskelion, the triple spiral at the very core of your nature. There are many ways of describing this treasure for you and walking the Sidhe-path in human life has made it possible for me to share it like this: *Be You, Be Gentle, Be Wild.* The order of the three is important as it reveals the most natural sequence of activation that will help you navigate in a healthy and balanced way with your life-unfoldment.

Being you is the art of coming home to yourself with renewed esteem for who and what you truly are, not just spiritually, but also personally and as part of a greater whole. This is the very first and crucial step to take when you embark on the journey of untaming you. Never leave this point of beginning untouched, as it will become the cornerstone of everything else. First and foremost, you must start embracing the fact that you are the missing piece to the puzzle. You are the sought-for world axis, the defining center, and if you leave yourself to seek elsewhere, all that matters will be futile. You need to be true to your own values, and you must be able to say yes and no, even to the most appealing guru in the world. Only thus you will be able to establish yourself as a reliable portal between worlds.

Many sincere seekers struggle immensely with this art of standing in one's own authentic being. Think about it. If you cannot honor yourself as a part of the universe, how can you truly honor anything else? You *are* the world, not separated but deeply connected, and when you start to own this deep truth, you can stand in your sovereignty, your inviolability. Then you gradually emerge as a leader in your own life.

 Being gentle is the art of opening to the heart space in the center of your being. As you grow in your ability to be you and not lose yourself in role playing, you allow a very gentle space to expand from your core. This is a natural and effortless unfolding that cannot be forced. It is all about allowing yourself to be with all that is, and to let things be. It is not a passive reaction. It is a participatory presence. First you need to let the gentleness rain upon your own affairs, like a soft shower. Then it will grow into recognizing the unique value of others and you start inviting partnership in wholeness.

This means that you engage in your world with tenderness and hospitality, learning new ways to become a good friend, a trusted family member and a treasured fellow human being. In the shared space of humaneness there is appreciation and respect. On this journey of combined authenticity and gentleness you will certainly discover how harsh you have been towards yourself and how much you have hurt others. However, discovering the fountain of compassion and empathy, stemming from your very own core, is the great safeguarding against misuse of power. It's the ethical sanctuary you should always honor.

Being gentle is a very simple thing and it goes for all affairs and situations in life: how you treat other living beings, how you take care of daily responsibilities and how you carry yourself. It is a work in progress, a constantly unfolding journey, and not about perfection. It is a state of your heart-mind that translates into your natural behavior: How you speak, think and feel. You do not repress and inhibit anything in yourself. Instead you allow a loving space more and more to hold everything within and around you. This art of gentleness is the second part of your life-triskelion, making you a natural healer in your own life.

 Being wild is the natural offspring of being you and being gentle, and it is incomparable with any kind of rough or savage blindness. Many people completely misunderstand wildness and reject it as something undeveloped. It is true that wildness can only be let loose in this respect when you have faced many hardships and challenges. This is what matures the heart and evolves the backbone of your robustness. It prepares you to allow wildness to enter. Wildness is engaging with the flow of the present. When you mount the wind of the moment you become the true dragon rider on the wave of creative imagination. It is to become the dancer in the land, and to move gracefully on the edge. Wildness is the gentle breeze in the early morning and the unfettered strokes of the wind in the autumn. It is the quivering flutter of a fragile butterfly, the whimsical glimpse in the eye of a stranger and the opening doors when craftmanship turns into true art. Wildness is not remote—it is right here in front of you. Nevertheless, this fact, gazing at you here and now, is something that many people avoid because they fear losing control.

How often do we dare to become spellbound by a unique moment? Do we stay with it or quickly return to so-called normality? Allowing yourself to marvel, to wonder and to whirl in the ever becoming present, is something that should not be a rare instant, and experienced from a deeper or higher perspective, it is a constant invitation from life to you and me. Beholding the fire of creation is to merge with the wild song of the ever becoming. It is to embark on the adventure of landing in the forgotten land. This is what we are all destined for and it isn't an exclusive right for the elected VIPs. Turned the other way around—there only exist VIPs and all are invited into the wildness.

We long for genuine authenticity, we long for gentleness, and we long for wildness. *Be you, be gentle, be wild*—this is the call that will answer the longing and help untaming us.

‿ GIFT ‿
Three Steps

Let yourself experience how it is to reclaim your dignity, your kindness and your inherent wildness. There are so many ways to start doing this, but here is a small menu you can use. It is highly recommended that you consider *authenticity* (being you), *kindness* (being gentle) and *creativity* (being wild) to be a wholeness—a triskelion— so when you focus on one of them, recognize that the two others are also potentially present. Here it is:

In a situation or during a challenge, decide to be **bravely honest**. Say things as they are. Don't camouflage it in any way. Be factual and direct if needed. Stand by yourself and do what is needed. While you attempt to be skillful in honesty by stating clearly how you perceive things, also invite kindness to be present so you honor the humane aspect of the situation and do not end up becoming harsh and cold. At the same time, allow a certain amount of openness to be present so you can adapt to changes.

In a situation or during a challenge, decide to be **kind-heartedly appreciative**. Emphasize the gentle and warmhearted angle that needs attention. Be calm and peaceful. Let it genuinely emanate from you as it is part of your nature. While you do your very best to practice this supportive and forthcoming way of being, be aware that you are also true and firmly rooted when you do it. Don't lose yourself in well-meaning "niceness" but be sure that you are true to yourself. Also give space to the improvising possibility so you are handling the situation with possible adjustments.

In a situation or during a challenge, decide to be **creatively spontaneous**. Open all your senses and give your full attention to what the situation demands. Often it is the inventiveness and the small, crazy suggestions that can loosen up a situation and offer new angles or opportunities. Suggesting brand-new and innovative approaches can be a great liberating force, if the involved parts are ready. While you engage with this refreshed awareness, remember to be empathetic and to have a real sense of what is needed in the situation, so you are not blown off-track by your love of novelties.

Practicing being you, being gentle and being wild is a great way of laying the foundation for your deeper and wider adventure. In fact, remembering to tend your Life-Triskelion is nothing less than hugely significant.

Seated Peacefully in the Wind

The Gaelic word *Sidhe* has very significant meanings that not only tell a story about our Sidhe-relatives, but ultimately point towards our inner Sidhe-nature as human beings.

Sidhe (Scottish Gaelic *"Sìth"*) literally means *mounds* or *hills*, referring to the sacred burial mounds and the palaces and residences that are beneath them in the Sidhe-realm in the "underworld"—the world under or behind ours. Interestingly in Norway a name for the Sidhe (the huldra people) is *the people of the hills* ("haugfolket"), again referring to the sacred hills in the landscape, mostly formed by humans in the past. These places are referred to as some of the homes of the Sidhe in Gaelic or Celtic tradition, and the Sidhe are recognized as seated or rooted there. Turning this within, Sidhe becomes a word for being seated, being placed or settled. This definitely refers to being in authority, being home, having fully landed in the right place—the foundation for life. Our inner Sidhe-nature starts to unfold when we are truly *seated* in our home within.

Sidhe also literally means *deep peace* as the Sidhe themselves have been known in tradition as *the people of peace*. This is hugely significant as we turn within and encounter Sidhe as the deeply rooted silence and power of peace. Resting in deep peace, anchored within yourself, unified with the gentle being of openness, is the gift of Sidheness, always saturated in the living connectedness with the greater wholeness. It is not just peace as the absence of noise and disturbances, but the deep peace in the ground of your being. The sense of being grounded and connected brings not only a solidity or a restful firmness, but also a tenderness and a sensitivity that is the hallmark of the heart.

Yet, there is another very important quality intimately related to the word Sidhe. In a note to his poem, *The Hosting of the Sidhe,* W. B. Yeats writes in *The Wind Among the Reeds:*

"Sidhe is also Gaelic for wind, and certainly the Sidhe have much
to do with the wind. They journey in whirling wind, the winds that
were called the dance of the daughters of Herodias in the Middle
Ages, Herodias doubtless taking the place of some old goddess.
When the country people see the leaves whirling on the road, they
bless themselves, because they believe the Sidhe to be passing by."

This specific quality of the wind is so clearly linking to wildness. The wind is always wild whether gentle or powerful. It cannot be tamed or regulated. Its very nature is unbound. To travel with the wind essentially is to connect with the heartbeat of freedom. Seated in our true identity, opening up to our peaceful, gentle presence, we experience the winds of freedom. When we are seated in the peaceful wind, we give ourselves over to the breath of life.

◌ Gift ◌
Follow the Wind

Give yourself the gift of going outside to feel the wind. Not just for a moment but take your time until you lose sense of time. Find a place where you can sit or stand comfortably. Start by focusing on how you can see what the wind does. The blowing force creates movements. You cannot see the wind itself, but you can see its impact. Trees are swaying, flags are waving. Perhaps a curtain is flapping. The wind is the great mover. It makes things change. The windy sea creates waves hitting the shores. The leaves are whirling up and down in spiraling patterns.

Now, listen to the sounds of the wind as it engages with buildings or wires in the air or leaves on the trees. It might be bells hanging in the tree or clothes being dried outside. There is an entire orchestra of wind music when we really pay full attention. Wind has a deep sound when it sweeps through a larger area, and lighter sounds when smaller things are affected by it.

As you keep seeing the movements from the wind and hear the many variations of sounds it brings forth, feel how the wind sweeps around you and touches your skin. Be fully aware of how it feels to be touched by the living, changing movements of the wind. It affects your whole body. You yourself become a wind resonator. By feeling the wind, you become part of the wind. You partake in the wind itself. With your being you *are* the wind, you *are* the free movement, you *are* the constantly moving aliveness. Stay in this as long as it feels natural. Let it affect you. Let it saturate you completely until you sense it is time to return to your normal presence. Notice what it does to you when you give in to the wind and join it with your undivided attention.

The Four Jewels

In order to go deeper into the mystery of our gentle wildness we need storytelling for a while. It is said that when the Humans and the Sidhe were separated, magic disappeared from the world. It was taken in custody by the Sidhe in their world, and the story goes that it was divided into four powers located in four different places, four distinct Sidhe-cities placed in the four corners of the world. They were carefully guarded and protected. These four powers are known as the four Hallows or the four Jewels. The four treasures are called:

The Stone of Destiny (also known as Lia Fáil, the Stone of Fal), placed in the city of Falias in the North, connected with the element of Earth. It is said that the stone will cry out in the presence of any true King.

The Cauldron of Plenty (also known as the Cauldron of Dagda), placed in the city of Murias in the West, connected with the element of water. It is said that no company will never leave it unsatisfied.

The Spear of Victory (also known as the Spear of Lugh), placed in the city of Finias in the South, connected with the element of fire. It is said that the Spear of Victory is invincible.

The Sword of Light (also known as the Sword of Nuada), placed in the city of Gorias in the East, connected with the element of air. It is said that the Sword of Light is irresistible, and no one can escape it.

The Four Hallows

Scarce information is given regarding these mystical objects, but to any keen observer it seems obvious that these four jewels are not to be seen as objects for a physical treasure hunt. We are not supposed to travel to exotic destinations to collect four items. Something much deeper is at play. The hint that the magic disappeared from the world is a clear allusion to the loss stemming from the division between Humans and Sidhe, but it is also mirrored in us as we have lost contact with something precious within ourselves.

At its core, the story about the four Hallows is connected to our own essence and to something we need to discover if deep magic is to be set free again. This requires that the separation between the Sidhe and Humanity ends, and it has a collective perspective as well as an individual perspective, namely that you and I start discovering our inner Sidhe-nature, our *Elvenforce*, leading to our innermost *Elvenheart*. From the four corners of our being we must collect the lost powers and bring them back to the center. The deepest buried secrets of being and growth are always within ourselves. Let us open the gates, walking the circle anti-clockwise to let a pattern unfold.

I

THE STONE-ANCHOR—THE FORGOTTEN POWER

Sovereignty, Leadership (Anchoring—Earth—North)
The Stone of Destiny is about Authority in life, reclaiming Sovereignty and discovering the nature of true Leadership.

The Stone of Destiny is about the destiny of every one of us, not just a few elected ones. It grants support to anyone when the time comes to own our true, royal nature and to stand by our responsibility and inherent authority. It is the foundation in anyone daring to stand in the power of flowing life. In order to make this happen we need to stay true to ourselves and to be genuine. This will give us access to steadfastness in life and to center our presence. Real leadership starts with our own life and it is not wishful thinking or role playing. It is the very core-identity of you and I, what we really are in our nakedness. The Stone is standing in North, connected with the very essence of the Earth and the robustness and immutable power that is the gift of anchoring.

Spiritually speaking the Stone of Destiny is the throne we sit upon when we have matured the courage to take ownership of being a leader in our own daily affairs. It is your destiny, and it is my destiny, to take our seat on the throne of leadership and sovereignty. We will do it many times as we start learning the art of leadership and natural authority. Ultimately it will culminate in distinct, visible leadership in whatever way is right for you. It is a crucial event as it will never go unheard but be proclaimed loudly—you step out of the crowd, the collective sea, and become visible. That's why the saying is that the stone "*cries out*" when true royalty approaches. You anchor in the ground of being and in the deep connectedness you stand erect in your land with dignity and appreciation. From there things can start happening. You and I contain this elusive, yet extremely powerful Stone-Anchor in the depths of our own nature.

II

THE FLOW-DANCER—THE FORGOTTEN CONNECTEDNESS

Abundance, Connection (Movement—Water—West)
The Cauldron of Plenty is about Reconnecting with Wholeness, discovering the natural dance of flow, flux and frolic—and revealing the nature of abundance and deep healing.

The Cauldron of Plenty satisfies the deepest thirst we have and bestows the discovery of the nourishing, renewing, recharging and life-giving support in all its facets. There is a quality of peaceful refreshment in this bowl or vessel of plenty and it is always reminding us of the deep connectedness of life as we do not drink of it as isolated individuals, but in fellowship or company. It satisfies and fulfils all longings, and because of this it is a deep, natural, healing source that brings renewal. The soft element of water and its flowing nature reminds us of the gentleness we are part of, and the ease we can align with in our daily living.

The Cauldron of Plenty has been associated with the Holy Grail, the source of spiritual life, eternally flowing with the waters of life, the blood or wine of love. From this cup of peaceful renewal, we can draw energy and inspiration to engage with the great flow of life. We transform from resting to moving activity as if our cup of joy is running over. There is a delight in this tender well of health, restoring our nature, and also a call to generosity and to engage with wholeness. The Cauldron of Plenty is the place for resting as well as the spring of gracefully flowing waters. We are invited to become nimble dancers of the valleys and hills of wholeness. You and I embody the Flow-Dancer emerging from this elusive, yet extremely powerful well of abundance.

III
THE FIRE-DREAMER—THE FORGOTTEN VISION

Hope, Intention (Imagination—Fire—South)
The Spear of Victory is about Reimagining Life, releasing the burning power of Hope and showing the pathways that bridge Heaven and Earth and leads to accomplishment.

The Spear of Victory embodies the power of triumph and invincibility. Its nature is to reach the goal and it fulfils the given purpose. Like a seagull arching from aloft and plunging itself into the sea to catch a fish, the spear is the creative imagination that finds a way from inner intention to outer expression. It mediates heaven and earth and makes the vision into reality. Flaming hope is an expression of purpose and creative improvisation that has merged. There is this mixture of one-pointedness and inventive adaptation to circumstances, bringing the inner intention to outer unfoldment. Therein lies victory and the optimistic resilience that is part of inner buoyancy. We need to reach the intended destination and realize the potential and possibilities within the seeds of promise.

The Spear has a burning quality as it points from above to below, but it is also full of the wild and ingenious movements of the flames. Within creative imagination lies a trust in life and a determination that inner perception will find a way to embodiment. On its way it undergoes a series of shapeshifting and adaptations as the weaving of wholeness is in the making. It is active in the South where the blossoming is full of fragrance and richness. The many sleeping seeds and spores have been revived and invited to growth by the generous warmth of the fiery sun. The Spear or lance is like a ray of flaming light, reaching from heaven to earth and from winter to bountiful summer. We can accomplish victory by leading the vision from possibility to realization. This will be a real triumph and a vindication of the deepest nature of flaming hope. You and I are the Fire-Dreamer in our very essence, and we are called to action.

IV
THE WIND-SINGER—THE FORGOTTEN SONG

Expression, Manifestation (Voice—Air—East)
The Sword of Light is about raising the voice and letting the sound of clarity and lucidity lead to the core of everything. From there the voice becomes the irresistible song of new life.

The Sword of Light holds the key to the irresistible and unavoidable power of life. This power is in the element of air and in the East where the sun rises. The air carries the sound—the East brings the light. The Sword cuts to the core and paves the way for that which cannot be withheld, and it commands by its very presence. It passes all obstacles to reach the core—the living essence of things. From there new life can manifest.

Metaphorically the Sword brings the clarity of the morning as the sun rises from the horizon and brings the brightness of daylight.

Everything is revealed in the voice. Like living tuning forks, we are meant to be acoustic resonators. Staying true to our own voice we can sound the notes that are truly ours. This requires that we use the sword of discrimination, the clarity of discernment, passing through all masks and outer appearances. Our true voice is heard in the air, vibrating and lucid, and its radiance finally becomes our life-song in the living, present now, resonating with the singing voices of all other singers in the great choir. The song that we are is released and it ascends from the deep, fragrant earth to the crystal-clear horizon in the forgotten, now rediscovered land. You and I are the Wind-Singers, liberating the forgotten tune and together we sing the new world into manifestation.

The four jewels are the four Hallows or treasures we all hold in the innermost parts of our being. They can be perceived like an almost forgotten mandala with a veiled and carefully protected ElvenHeart in the center.

4
SEEKING THE ELVENHEART

Searching for Heartland

Let me invite you on a journey, an adventure that may open the doors to your four jewels and gradually unravel the nature of your Elven-Heart. We are not used to finding out that fairy tales are real. Our modern world with its complexities and challenges does not seem to fit neatly with such a perspective. All fairy tales originate from reality and it would serve us well if we embraced this fact.

Imagine that there is a magical Heart Stone in the essence of your being, infused with glittering starlight and Gaian abundance. It has been said that the Sidhe-Heartland on the planet is at a place called *Glen of Precious Stones* with a Ruby Heart at its center. It lies in the Emerald world of Gaia, and the saying goes that all the Sidhe visit this place to renew their life. This beautiful story is about any Heartland: We need to renew ourselves by opening up to the very heart of our being. In searching for wholeness, we might get a deep feeling or sense that this does not just refer to a place on the planet, but to something within you and me.

Consider the following journey to be a practical guide. I will share it with you also as a personal voyage and in a very special way we will use the breath as our lifeline. Think for a moment how easy it is to calm down and get more in contact with yourself. You simply have to remember your breath and stay with it. So, the beginning of our journey is to search for the breath.

The Beginning

Your very first breath at birth is taking in the air outside your mother, often followed by your first sound—sometimes a cry, letting the sound be set free into the world: you have arrived! There will come a moment that will be the last moment of your life in this world. If listened to with care, it will be the sound of your final exhalation followed by silence: you have left the building.

Everything between these two monumental events is what we call living a life: more than seven million smaller breaths each year of your life in an unfolding story with countless moments and innumerable events, learning and growth, a mystery to be lived, a magic to be experienced, a challenge to face and a wonder to unfold.

Your life is unique. No one has ever lived it before. No one can live it again. It is fragile, powerful, and precious—your life—with all its crises and tribulations, in all its beauty and goodness. The very beginning of your journey here is an inhalation, a breathing in of fresh air, followed by an announcement with a signature belonging only to you: "*I am here!*" And yes, you and I and all other beings—we are here, and each one of us is incredibly miraculous.

It is sometimes said that beginnings are small. In fact, all beginnings are small. Think about this: the most incredible miracles, the greatest outcomes, and stunning events all start in tiny ways. The very first drops are followed by a small stream of water. Later, it is a refreshing current that grows into a flood. Finally, it is an unstoppable, roaring river forcing its way towards the ocean.

This journey is meant to be a drop—it is a possible beginning. Applied in life, it might become part of a stream that makes a clear difference and sets many things in motion. Everything that really means something has the nature of a domino effect. Give the drop a chance to do its work and many things will come from it. Breathe your life into it and it will answer as a gentle wind full of wonders. Consider this book to be a journey that is also a search for life's treasures. It is all about life—the wondrous, incredible, miraculous reality you are right in the midst of. Exactly where you are, there is a living breath pulsating to its own rhythm. Lean into it. Listen to it. Learn from it.

Where to start? I propose that we give a moment's attention to timeless wisdom from experienced sources. For ages, people have lived and shared the greater life we are part of, and their observations support each other in surprising ways.

Lending an Ear

Religious and spiritual traditions contain many references to the divine or spiritual as the essence of breath, air, or wind, and the physical reflection is shown in our breathing as well as in the wind itself. The Greek word *pneuma* means breath, air, or wind, and is also used as an equivalent for spirit, the very breath of life. In Christian tradition, it is the word used to signify The Holy Spirit, the emanation from the Lord (Hebrew: *ruach*, Aramaic: *rucha*). In Buddhism, the soul is sometimes referred to as *"wind horse"* and the life-giving winds are part of both Buddhist and Hindu traditions. The creative sound is the vibration of spirit in Christian (Greek: *logos*), Hindu (Sanskrit: *aum*), and Tibetan (*lung*) tradition, and similar meanings can be found in other traditions. In the Gospel of John (3:8), Jesus says: *"The wind [pneuma] blows where it wishes and you hear the sound of it, but do not know where it comes from and where it is going; so is everyone who is born of the Spirit [pneuma]."*

You and I are living expressions of the wind of spirit or life itself. The wind is always in movement, as is life. No matter how quiet we become, there is always some kind of movement. Movement has sound, and sound vibrates in the air, the air we breathe. Being alive means that we inhale and exhale, and the rhythm is part of the great cycle of life—also expressed in the circadian rhythm, the changing between day and night, the yearly cycle, and the grand rhythmic cycle of the planets circling the Sun and the Moon as they orbit the Earth. Everything inhales and exhales in a ceaseless ritual of renewal and repetition. So, breath is everywhere. It is the sound of Mother Nature, blowing in the trees, murmuring in the waves, whispering in the leaves, and echoed in the utterances from all living beings through their vocal organs and organisms. The Earth itself breathes in all its cycles and changes. Nature teaches us to be part of the great flow, the respiratory system of interactive ecology we call the living Earth.

Life Is Wild—But What about You?

If you try to catch and hold life in a fixed position, it escapes or eludes you. Like a fragile butterfly or a rare bird bereft of sunlight, or a powerful creature tamed and living in predictable captivity, something will soon be missing, and the essence exits the scene, leaving only a shell behind. In many cases, spirit breaks free from the entrapped form and finds other places to live. Life can be held for a moment, but it cannot be trapped perpetually.

This is universal. Such is life. We cannot tell where the wind comes from or where it goes. We cannot control the wind, for it is the living breath of the creative spirit. Thank God we are not in control! We must let go of the constant craving to be in command and desperately uphold an inflexible regulation. Life cannot be contained in predictable boxes and anticipated structures. It will always surprise and find its way out, one way or another. What an incredible blessing! We are not meant to be tamed and predictable, boring and colorless. Our very human nature is nature itself in unfoldment.

However, we seem to have forgotten this basic truth. We have gained so much during evolution, but we have also blinded ourselves and lured our attention into an almost lifeless condition of comfort-seeking tameness. We are not meant to be domesticated in our consciousness. Habits are necessary, but they are meant to help us, not turn us into dull beings by confining our nature. We are caught up in the survival game of *"fight, flight, and freeze,"* yet we are so much more than these anxiety triggers that try to cope with a possible danger. Instead of being freely active, full of wonder and curiosity, we often tend to get caught up in reacting all the time in a defensive way. Either we resist or fight the opposing powers, or we flee the scene in fear of ending in defeat and captivity. If these two strategies do not work, we freeze and hope that invisibility will somehow help us to survive in the jungle of life.

There is, however, a great beauty and truth to be discovered behind the three Fs. After all, we are so much more than these diminutive notes on the grand tone scale we are part of. Fighting shows that we possess great power, flight displays our great sensitivity, and freeze is evidence of our inherent and great intelligence. When we step back and stand in our true being, we dare to acknowledge the authority and sovereign power we are always subject to. When we realize that flight is due to our emotional awareness and longing for safety, we begin to become aware that the safest harbor is the loving heart that embraces everything. In the same way, when we start observing the impulse to freeze, we begin to understand that here lies a rudimentary brightness, an ability to intelligently read the signs of life and witness that everything is part of a grand and meaningful design. Fight, flight, and freeze can therefore become door-openers into a much larger presence that is always at hand—simply because it is part of what we are, and not just what we have. You and I are power, love, and intelligence—and we do have conditions that can make us withdraw and respond to a threat with the strategies of fight, flight, and freeze.

Are you wild in a wonderful way? Do you give in to fight, flight, or freeze as the game of life, or have you started unraveling the hidden treasure behind the well-known territory of so-called normality? Are you afraid to be called insane if you leave the well-trodden highways of accepted sanity?

The Loss

As a spiritual presence, you are born wild and meant to stay wild. Nevertheless, there is a huge journey from the unconscious wildness in your early and often protected childhood to the consciously conquered wildness in your matured adulthood. Most people get caught up in the lame-tame game between these two forms of wildness. The unconscious wildness is blind and instinctual, but also innocent as a childhood phase. There is nothing wrong with it. It is natural and immediate, aware in the present moment. This first wildness is like an element of nature acting entirely in accordance with its inherent constitution. It is wrong to call a child selfish as it is exploring and learning. We have all been there and know its basic components: craving, delight, enjoyment, curiosity, satisfaction, and—most importantly—no judgment. Things are what they look like.

Gradually, we are socialized and learn to adapt to cultural norms. We grow up and mature. This is the journey from the wilderness of infancy into the imitation game, where we gradually learn how to survive with the tribe, with our family, our history, our environment, and our society. Step by step, we are initiated into the predictable world of intellectual structure and rationality. Numerous things are learned, skills are developed, and we become self-conscious. During this extensive phase, we evolve as calculating and controlling individuals. We step out of paradise and enter the world of structured domination. We gain a great deal: the ability to master and navigate in a complicated realm, and the qualities of self-confidence, focused concentration, and stamina. We adapt and improvise, but more than anything else, we expand the platform of becoming self-conscious beings with a distinctive personality.

In this whole process, we also lose contact with our past. We cut off the instinctual part of ourselves and let go of it in favor of intellectual reason and common sense. In the long run, we end up getting lost in the maze of semi-conscious tameness. Fear plays a great part, simply because we cannot control everything, no matter how hard we try. In the process, we inhibit the emotional signals and struggle with insecurity and confusion. Intellect cannot save us from disaster. We are in some kind of control, and yet we lose it again and again.

Think about it for a moment. How much do you hold yourself back in your daily activities and avoid doing things that you would really like to do? How much do you adapt and compromise? I am not talking about following every kind of impulse at any moment. I am simply pointing at the restraint we put on ourselves and each other, mostly without saying anything. We follow public opinion, the cultural patterns of our society, and the socializations we have been molded by. When someone does unusual things, most people react by shaking their heads, mocking them, or ignoring the event as something inappropriate or immature. The fact is that the main factor behind these reactions is fear, and so the comfort zone of "*business as usual*" wins out. The deviator is often the brave heart that creates a pathway to renewal, and we should praise it as a highly needed role model. What frequently happens, however, is that the unusual activities are bashed and rejected.

Today, we acutely need renewal by means of the redeeming quality of wildness. Wildness is the hope of the world. We need the wind of renewal as much as we need sunshine and oxygen to live, and yet most of us content ourselves with the breadcrumbs of plastic civilization, copycat mentality, and surrogate happiness. We could have a life of incredible magic and abundance, and yet we often accept tiny boxes filled with artificial stuff. We long for more life yet fear to live. To put it differently: we suffer from existential claustrophobia, yet we are infected with agoraphobia—we are tired of our tiny space yet fear to get more space. And this is where awakening begins.

Early Awakening

I clearly remember a sense of being divided in my childhood, one part of me playing the game, learning the tricks of survival, and adapting to the expected. It helped me a lot, and I later learned how to pass school exams with flying colors, simply because I played the game. The other part of me was observing and asking what was going on. Was this life? Was I supposed to mingle and play my roles without asking what all this was about? Could this masquerade be the whole story? Could there not be a greater purpose behind the hide-and-seek of so-called normality? At the age of five, I was deeply moved at the sight of golden eagles and felt a spiritual ecstasy of upliftment without having words for it. At seven, while sitting on my favorite stone in the garden, I would wonder what great mystery lay behind everything. And by the time I was twelve, I was seriously questioning the deeper meaning of life and asking my parents what they were thinking. I got no answers from others. I had to keep diving deep within myself.

My social nature helped me to survive my teenage years, and yet I felt alone with my observations and had to write poems and make abstract drawings to keep the inner realm alive. Most of it I kept to myself. I came through puberty with a lot of surrogates and learned the survival game of conformity. It was fun and it was boring. It was exciting and it was trivial. I started smoking, drinking, and driving fast on my moped in my leather jacket and high-heeled boots—the fashion style of the mid-seventies. I learned many lessons and matured. It was part of growing older and it was natural and meaningful in its own way. Nevertheless, a part of me was awaiting the larger life beyond the borders of predictability.

When I was seventeen, I awoke to the greater reality simply by accidentally stumbling upon the word *theosophy*—divine wisdom— in an encyclopedia. I was struck by recognition without knowing what it meant. I soon found out, and a few years later, I had to follow the clarion call of becoming a spiritual teacher—very young, in many ways not ready, yet ready enough to dare doing it. And so, my tiny beginning got underway in the midst of a young life. I was touched by the winds of something larger than my daily, conscious "I"—and at the same time knew I was part of it.

Since you are reading this, I am sure you have your own version of how you awoke to something greater than the humdrum of flatland. We all experience our shift from one phase to another, and if you are reading this, I am sure you have had your changes, jumping from one level to another.

Let me be very clear. Awakening to something greater does not in any way mean that daily life is unimportant. On the contrary: daily life *is LIFE*. What is crucial is how you and I perceive it, and whether we think the socialized norms and habitual patterns of our local culture is *ALL* there is. If innocence and wonder have left the building and we are left behind with the cynical and toxic "reality" of a brutal morass and a surface existence of prestige, image, and charades, we are surely better off with something completely different. Here, the door may open for a pleasant surprise.

Reclaim the Sweetness

Unconscious wildness is our shared inheritance. Controlled rationality is the predominant presence in our civilization today. Ahead of us lies conscious wildness and it is beginning to show. The simple difference between the three is this:

Unconscious Wildness	Rational Consciousness	Conscious Wildness
Instinct	Intellect	Intuition

We learn from everything. Our instinctual past is indispensable and laid the foundation for the mental unfoldment we are part of today. Instinct enables us to react immediately when facing a possible danger, while intellect allows us to plan for future survival and to develop many practical skills. Instinct is the immediate response to stimuli. Intellect is the reflective, self-conscious process of controlling and mastering innumerable things, as well as the possibility to understand and realize. Both abilities are partners in life and well-doers in our lives if they exist peacefully side by side. In our present situation, however, they are often at war against each other. Our gut feelings say one thing, but our mind tells us something entirely different, resulting in conflict.

We often let the domesticated, habitual, and repetitive mind conquer and dominate, and down in the basement, where our gut feelings reside, the instincts roar, sometimes boiling up and erupting into scary flares or explosions, disrupting the agreeable surface of ordinary life. Think about your own life: you think about something and perhaps convince yourself that it is OK, and at the same time you feel it is wrong. What do you do in such a situation? How do you solve the puzzle? It is the classical drama between sense and sensibility. Is the mind entirely wrong and are our feelings telling the complete truth?

I think we can agree that the mind and our emotional nature both have their role to play but if we are trapped in the tension between intellect and instinct, we continue to miss something essential. This is where conscious, intuitive wildness—the saving grace of our greater being—comes into the picture. It is the missing dimension in our lives. That's why we need to reclaim wildness, not repeat the past of instinctual awareness or the well-known intellectual domination. We need to give way to the living breath of life, the wind that carries joy and innocence into the equation, the key to rediscovering the natural effortless way of being what we are capable of, and the freedom and redeeming sweetness of spirit full of light, love, and power. There is a pathless path to this wonder of life. It lies right in front of you and me. It can be described and taught in innumerable ways. Let me invite you to a very simple yet profoundly deep approach. You already know something about it, but now we will revisit it and let it unfold.

Four Portals to Your ElvenHeart

Consider your life journey to be an adventure towards revival, a grand hike towards awakening. Every step you take on this epic journey has the deeper purpose of waking up to who you are and what you are here to do. Your story is yours alone, but at the same time it is also a universal drama unfolding through your life, carrying a flavor of uniqueness. No one but you will ever walk in your shoes right here and right now. Your story of a more profound awakening will never be repeated. Your piece in the grand jigsaw of life is one of a kind and therefore particularly precious. You bring to the table an indispensable part of the living tapestry of life.

This means that you must find your own way. You cannot copy others. They can inspire you but never show you exactly what to do or how to do it. By living your life more and more consciously with a living awareness and a heartful presence, you will inevitably chance upon the keys or doors to more abundance, joy, and meaningful existence. You are here to discover who you are, what you bring with you, and how you can accomplish it. In the process, you will find out how to have a life with a home and with purposeful activities. You will also learn the art of relating to others, unfolding your heart with kindness and compassion, and weaving your skills into the great fabric of the larger world you are part of. You are here to learn to act, love, and create exactly in the way that makes sense to you according to your nature and your passion. This is your business. This is your exclusive story. This is your epic journey of becoming alive—to reclaim a lost paradise and become the wild wind of the spirit.

There are countless ways to show the way on this journey. Only you will know what appeals to your keynote, brings glow to your eyes, and opens your heart. Let us walk together for a while, and hopefully I can inspire you to discover or attune to your odyssey towards a new dawn.

I

THE STONEANCHOR—YOUR STONE OF DESTINY

The first portal we call the StoneAnchor and it is deeply grounded in the earth. It is the fact that you must first be true to yourself. In the words of Shakespeare: *"This above all: to thine own self be true"* (Hamlet: Act 1, Scene 3). You will never accomplish anything that is true if you do not rely on your own value. This is the foundation stone of the true journey of your awakening, your destiny.

II
THE FLOWDANCER—YOUR CAULDRON OF PLENTY

The second portal we call the FlowDancer. It flows, ripples, and rushes like glittering water. It is the fact that as you gradually become more rooted in the being you really are, you will be invited to step out into the river of life and let yourself be moved. This makes you alive in new ways. You unfold your playfulness and become much more effortless, spry, and swift. You open the heart and share your cauldron of plenty.

III
THE FIREDREAMER—YOUR SPEAR OF VICTORY

The third portal we call the FireDreamer. It glows, flares, and blazes like warm and transforming fire. It is the fact that you are destined to be a creative dreamer in the living world of imagination, the stuff that molds the reality of tomorrow. This is the wonder of dreaming impossible dreams and awakening to the wonderful potentials in the stream of life. This is the flaming hope, bringing heaven to earth, your spear of victory.

IV
THE WINDSINGER—YOUR SWORD OF LIGHT

The fourth portal we call the WindSinger. It vibrates, sounds, and resonates in the breeze. It is the fact that when you are learning to navigate in the flow of life, firmly rooted in your nature, it is time to find your voice and attune to the greater song of life. This enables you to be heard, and you vocalize and express your creativity in an expanding harmony with the greater whole. This is the Sword of Light, vibrating like a crystal star in the bountiful land of your life.

The four portals hold the honey, or nectar, that nurtures us on the path of becoming the untamed breath of the spirit, unfolding the mysterious ElvenHeart at the core of our humanity. You and I are WindSingers in the living breath. We are FireDreamers, FlowDancers and StoneAnchors. This is our living mandala, our real nature—these are the four faces of breath, awaiting our coming.

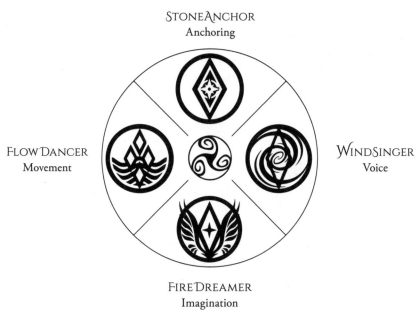

STONEANCHOR
Anchoring

FLOWDANCER
Movement

WINDSINGER
Voice

FIREDREAMER
Imagination

The Four Portals

◦ GIFT ◦
The Non-Exercise

Life today is so full of agendas, deadlines, and things to accomplish. This easily takes over in spiritual approaches as well and you end up repeating the very same things you wanted to let go of.

Here is an exercise that is no exercise. It is so simple. It even let's go of exercising. It is a return to the most essential part of being alive. Sometimes, we seem so far from what is most obvious, the simplest we can imagine. In a way, it is a switch-off. We rarely switch off. We are online most of the time. Now you can do the opposite—or undo it.

Just sit relaxed. You may be alone, but you can do this even if you are not completely alone. If you have your smartphone with you, turn it off. If there are other devices that may try to get your attention, turn them off. Now, switch yourself off. Let go of having to do anything. Just sit. If your eyes are open, let go of any focus. Defocus. Just experience that you are. Don't focus on any specific body part. Experience your whole body. Sense it. Sense your presence permeating your whole body. Experience that you are awake. If thoughts emerge, let them be. If feelings arise, let them be. Experience the beating of your heart. It simply beats. You don't need to do anything at all. You are pausing. You are fully allowed to pause. You don't need to think about anything. You are allowing yourself to do nothing at all. You are sitting relaxed. Your heart beats. You are.

Experience your breath. No need to regulate it. The breath has its own pulse, its own rhythm, just like the heart. You are simply relaxing, experiencing the pure enjoyment of being awake and not needing to do anything. You don't do—you are. Take your time—forget time. Experience the utterly simple presence of being. Let go of any formula—even the formula of this non-exercise. You are not following any routine. You are not exercising. You are re-entering your primal presence. You are breathing. Your heart beats. Your body is. You are.

Give yourself the freedom to create this switch-off. Give yourself this pure pausing. You came into this life naked and with absolutely no calculation or emotional agenda in your mind or your feelings. You were like a clear presence not yet molded or socialized. You didn't respond to expectations or conscious memories. You simply arrived. You inhaled and exhaled. There was light, movement, sensing, presence—and you arrived. You left the womb of embracing darkness, came out into the light and this life began. There was a creative intent from your inner source, and you came here to manifest and play, but it all began with a simple arrival. No agenda. Just arrival, fresh and pure.

The non-exercise can be experienced as a return to what is simplest and most fundamental: to breathe and to be. To feel the heartbeat and the living bodily presence. To awaken—letting go of all attachments, pure and simple.

Enjoy the non-exercise from time to time. Let it permeate you, effortlessly. Let go of trying anything. Let everything be. Breathe and be. Just be. Do it as long as you find it right to do so. Then gradually return to your outer focus and the activities you are part of.

5

THE STONEANCHOR

You left yourself to discover everything else.
You exhausted your energies on a voyage to a faraway land,
Meandering, hoping, finding everything else but yourself.
Now it is time to come back.
Stand firmly on your ground.
Come home.
Be you.

Standing Stone

One would think that the most elemental thing in the world is to be oneself. Everything else around us can seem very complicated, but the simple awareness of being who you are—this cannot be rocket science. And yet it seems that in many ways, we have left ourselves to such a degree that we have developed a numbness of self-presence. This is nothing new. In his 1841 essay *Self-Reliance*, the American writer and philosopher Ralph Waldo Emerson repeatedly encourages us to trust ourselves. Many of his words are highly relevant today, not least when he emphasizes: *"To be yourself in a world that is constantly trying to make you something else is the greatest accomplishment."*

And here we are, you and I, with the possibility of coming home to our own base. This is not as simple as it may sound. The tendency to avoid looking within is buried deep in our psyche and mind. Not least among people who work holistically and spiritually, there is often a lack of self-care. Deep down in their subconscious, many of them despise and loathe themselves even as they are engaged in trying to heal others. This is a self-contradiction. It is like trying to love a cake while hating its ingredients. Everything that involves you also carries the qualities of your being. The very idea of being "pure" indicates that you are dirty and often hides a self-hatred or at least an inability to be kind to yourself. You cannot be a "pure channel" if it means being taken out of the equation. It is like saying that the riverbed does not affect the flow of the water. We are meant to qualify and color what comes through us. We are not here to be absent. We are here to be present in the world and to bless it with our presence, and it involves all that we are and hold within us. We are not neutral containers. We are unique gifts and we need to appreciate this fact.

Trying to escape from yourself, seeking atonement and salvation from external authorities makes no sense. The only way you can forgive others is by forgiving yourself. When something good and kind reverberates from your center, its ripples will carry the authenticity everybody talks about. Therefore, you need to be genuinely kind to yourself. The words spoken by Jesus: *"Love your neighbor as yourself"* (Matt. 22:39; Mark 12:30) mean that you are your own neighbor. The love you give to others, you must give yourself. This may sound like a trivial truth you have heard many times before, but how do you practice it? Many people ignore the obvious and wear themselves out trying to please others so that they will be loved. Yet they forget to do the simplest things for themselves. Service to others can be a hiding game. The price is heavy. Therefore, take yourself seriously—with gentleness.

This is a very difficult journey for many people, and it may imply that help from others is needed. You may need to receive assistance and care from others to gradually discover that you have been a refugee fleeing from your own home. Now you need to return and discover that the greatest treasure always lies buried right where you stand. You will not find the gem of life anywhere else. It is right in your center. Recognizing this can mark a great turning point as you start the journey of returning home. You need to embrace yourself with all that you contain. In this opening up to self-worth, you may feel able to honor yourself in exactly the same way that you honor and appreciate others. You can begin to face up to all the excuses you have used for not standing up for yourself, and for not defending your values and your dignity as a human being.

How many times have you let yourself down? How often have you betrayed the value of being you and tried to please others? Do you know the feeling of being hard on yourself? Do you feel uncomfortable when others praise you? If any of this sounds familiar, it becomes clear that gentleness towards yourself is very important. In fact, a fully reversed journey may begin, namely the gentle approach to the deep appreciation of who you are.

You are the standing stone in the grand circle of your life. You need to stand in all your dignity, upright and relaxed. You need to experience how you can breathe freely, deep down into your stomach, with a feeling of being in the right place, exactly where you are. It is crucial that you discover the importance of establishing a center within yourself. If there is no clear center, everything is potentially in chaos and you cannot navigate in life. Instead, you are tossed around like driftwood on a stormy ocean. As soon as you establish your core, everything around you starts to reconfigure. You become visible as a clear keynote in the cacophony of the world. It might sound very exaggerated when you consider your daily doings, your family relations, and social circles, but it works. The drop becomes the stream and over time, if nurtured, it evolves into the powerful river. All gigantic shifts start in tiny ways from within. When you can acknowledge the fact that you are a significant force in the world, you will know as a fact that this is reality.

Childhood Stone

When I was a child, I lived in a house with a big garden, and on the lawn, there was a big stone, supported by smaller stones and a bush. I loved to sit on the stone. It was my sweet spot for dreaming and connecting with the living world around me. I loved to play and run around, but I was also a dreamer, especially on my big stone in the garden. When I was sitting there, I felt it was natural to connect with the trees, birds, and living creatures around me. In a way, I was centered. I could turn around on the stone and every angle offered a good view. During the warm months, I would also use the stone as a place to jump from, and in June, around my birthday, the flowering bush, a Chamaecytisus, would display its gorgeous flowers and give me that yellow feeling of the sunny side of life. In the evenings, around sunset, I would listen to a blackbird singing in trees close by and turn towards the west or north. Then I would dream of the larger reality behind the outer forms and feel like a child of the stars and nature.

It is remarkable how deep feelings of connectedness can go, and how much a single spot can mean. I was a loved and very social child, so the stone was not an escape from a harsh reality. On the contrary. In my safe world, the stone was like a centering place to connect with the greater wholeness, the mysterious world I was part of. We moved to another place when I was a teenager, but more than three decades later, I felt a need to visit the house. Luckily, the present owners opened their doors to me and let me revisit the garden. Right there, still on the lawn, was the stone, and I was able to sit on it once again and reconnect to the timeline in my life. It is clear to me that the stone was a symbolic core in the life of my searching spirit and my sense of coming home to a center. Since then, I have enjoyed other stones to sit, stand, or lie on. Perhaps there are certain places in your life that once held a similar meaning for you in your early years, or still mean something to you today. They could be anywhere: a tree, a room, a meadow, a chair, or a corner in a coffee shop? Objects or places sometimes become our partners in the centering process. Realizing their significance can help you to open up to what anchoring means to you, and how it can evolve.

Break or Breathe

Taking your position as the standing stone in your world is not something that will go unnoticed. Sooner or later, it will generate great opposition. You will be tested. This is the only way you can make it evolve into something powerful. It is not a sudden whim, but a decision that must grow within you, and as it gains momentum, it will be tested. It is neither wrong nor bad, but a law of nature. Everything that grows will meet resistance. It is part of the "weather conditions" of every leap in consciousness that there will be tranquility for a period and then turmoil for a period. The wind will die down and give way to warmth and sunshine. Then clouds will gather, and the gentle breeze will grow into a storm that sweeps across the landscape of your life. No one can avoid this cyclic change. There will be testing.

When you come to understand testing as a fact of life, and your foundation needs to be expanded, you will begin to accept that you will occasionally seem to lose ground because of the opposition you face. It may come from others, from your surroundings, or from within yourself—or from a combination of these things. If you fight this with resistance, you might go through a hurtful phase, one that causes many wounds. But if you observe the energy in the resistance and start accepting that it is trying to teach you something, things will probably turn out much better for you. In its easier varieties, it is a matter of disruption or release; in its most radical expressions, one of breakdown or upliftment.

In all this, you can choose how to react. There is always a choice: break or breathe! If you choose fight, flight, or freeze as strategies of survival, things could end up pretty bad for you as you try to deny what's going on. As the famous catchphrase from Star Trek goes: "*Resistance is futile.*" You can give in or cave in, let go or capitulate. If you choose to let go and accept that resistance is actually fruitless, you will not break, but breathe. Energy will come to you because you have given up the very idea of mastering and managing from your usual control panel. Learning to anchor your energy and manifest the standing stone demands that you surrender to a greater force than your mind. You must step back and let in more energy. This may look like the raising of a white flag, but in reality, it is to allow something bigger to enter the scene. I can give you an example from my own life.

Earthquaked

In 2017, I was earthquaked. My life as spiritual teacher, coach, and author was going very well. I was happily married and felt I was on the top of my life. I didn't see the tsunami coming until it hit me. It was totally unexpected, and my safe harbor fell apart. In all my almost thirty years of married life, I had never flirted, never fantasized about another relationship. My wife was the best friend, life companion, and mentor I could imagine. I was exactly where I was supposed to be. I was grateful, my life was rich, and I was full of plans, following my present track. And yet, one day, I received an email that shook my world. It was very straightforward, a warm mail like thousands of other mails I had received as a teacher. It was a mail thanking me for my work. And yet—in a way I could not, and still cannot fully explain—it was as if a forgotten sound had crept past all my defenses and landed gently in the center of my being. The (to me) unknown sender had attached a song to the mail in the form of an audio file. After reading the respectful and warm mail, I opened the file and listened to the song.

I was profoundly moved and noticed that I had been holding my breath. I will add that what I experienced at the time was a deep soul recognition that passed all the layers of mind and emotions and went right to my core. This person—whom I did not know and had never met, and who was simply thanking me for my activities—spoke to my being in a way that defied all explanation. It was a tremor, a silent shock that hit me below or behind any confidence or conviction I possessed, and which I registered as a feeling of unrest, as something that moved me beyond words, only after I had read the mail and listened to the song.

What followed is the personal story of a world collapsing, shaken in a way that perhaps makes sense only to the one experiencing it. I remember that, just two days later, I took up an invitation from my friend Jeppe Hein and visited him in Berlin. I simply had to play the song for him and mention my strange kindred spirit in Denmark. He listened to it and nodded. It was a good singer. Even now as I write these words, the very song, based on a poem by the Irish author and poet William Butler Yeats, is the story of a deep longing. It is called *The Song of Wandering Aengus* and tells the story of an old man remembering how he met a beautiful girl in his youth—not a normal human being, but a female faery, or Sidhe, who appeared before him transformed from a trout he had just caught in the stream. The glimmering girl with apple blossom in her hair called him by his name and ran and faded through the brightening air. Someone also "*called me by my name*" but the person did not fade away. Three months later, I had to capitulate and five months later, I was divorced. I was open with my wife from day one and did not start an affair. Nothing was secret and I was in despair. For three months, I recited: "*But I am happily married! But I am happily married! But I am happily married*"—yet my marriage collapsed.

This may sound like a trivial story about falling in love and leaving the spouse, something countless people go through—so what's the point here? It's very simple—and deeply complex. I was struck to my core even before I got to know the person. And before I knew it, a fire broke out, consuming the foundation of my personal life. Yes, I fell in love. Yes, I was struck by the other person, fascinated— drawn to this human being like metal to a magnet. But the story was about recognition, a deep sense of congeniality—of meeting an *Anam Cara*—a soul friend—as they say in Irish Gaelic. It was about meeting a partner, a friend, an alter ego—someone already deeply loved. I was earthquaked and the personal foundation of my private life was shaken into pieces. I lost my ground—I was scared like never before—and I had to start on a completely new journey from scratch.

Rebuilding from the Ground

We all have our unique forms of collapse when something must end abruptly and something new begins. It is like holding your breath. I held mine, and then I had to face what I was in the middle of. According to logion 2 of the Gospel of Thomas, Jesus said: *"Let him who seeks continue seeking until he finds. When he finds, he will become troubled. When he becomes troubled, he will be astonished."* The Danish translation says the seeker will become shaken. This universal truth may find innumerable expressions and at many levels depending on the personal circumstances. Each situation is unique and cannot be repeated or copied. I was troubled and astonished at the same time when life called me to unexpected change and renewal.

I was shaken to the core, for I thought I knew myself. After the divorce, I felt deep guilt and sorrow. I didn't seek this earthquake, yet it found me in the form of a soul I recognized to a degree that I was unable to deny. In the midst of my great fear, I had to follow the courage that arose, trusting my innermost feelings with no guarantees of anything. I had to leave my beloved partner of thirty-three years, the mother of our two adult girls. I had to rely on a compass needle pointing into the seemingly unknown, move to another part of the country, take a driver's license for the first time at the age of fifty-six, live in two basements for a year, and start building a new life with the soul who had been equally struck by the clarion call.

It was extremely difficult, and I cried more in the year after the separation than I had ever cried before in my entire life. Besides developing a love relationship with my new partner and teaching with her as an equal colleague—which we were really good at—I also had to develop a relationship with her three-year-old daughter, grow into the role of a "bonus father," and learn to adapt to entirely new challenges of daily life. It was definitely not my home turf. At times, I felt incredibly weak and questioned my own sanity. Yet in spite of the sorrow, the way I had hurt my ex-wife and shocked my two daughters, and how I had gone into something seemingly crazy and not very clever—I knew in my bones that I had done the right thing. Throughout all this, I had to affirm the love and recognition that called my new partner and me together and to stand by my deepest sense of what appeared to be a true call to more life.

When a new foundation is being established, we will often face fear and uncertainty. I have faced it and you will know what I am talking about if you have experienced anything similar. It may, for example, be in the form of a financial upheaval, illness, death, betrayal, or love. Whatever form it takes, it will test you, but it is also an invitation to something completely new. You may feel a deep loss, profoundly disturbed, numb, or naked, but you will also be able to feel the new, fresh breath of life blowing into your garden, felling trees that cannot stand firm. I needed to hold my ground and let the attachments go. So do you. What cannot stand will fall. This is the nature of the tornado from the breath of life when we are called to renewal. It is tough but can be truly liberating. It comes with a price and it comes with a gift. They belong together. *Everything depends not on how we feel, but how we take it.*

During this process, I have often felt like a Stone Age man trying to rediscover the fire in my own life. At times, I have been desperate, and I am sure nothing would have made sense if love had not been there from the very beginning. Only the most precious could have brought me out on a limb like this. There may come a time when we all need to reinvent the wheel in our own lives, simply because the present condition—no matter how safe and nice it seems to be—has become a sedative or a hindrance. I still love my ex-wife and feel heavy and full of sorrow whenever I contemplate the pain I have caused her by my decision to leave. She is not to blame, and she did not deserve my course of action. I destroyed her world but could not help it. I must live with my decision and accept all it has invoked. However, I know I could not have done otherwise without betraying my innermost being. I have learnt entirely new things about vulnerability, guilt, and uncertainty, but I have also learned new things about courage, readiness, and love.

The Rock of Presence

To encounter the new and unblemished, you need to leave behind everything you know, to experience the condition of feeling homeless in order to be able to come home. This archetypal journey of awakening is described in many fairy tales, myths, and legends. Once upon a time everything was idyllic and surrounded by fortified comfort zones. Then the peace was disturbed, and a horrible battle ensued, with opposing powers smashing against the cornerstones of "business as usual." Finally, the epic confrontation resulted in victory, enabling the hero or heroine—or both—to inaugurate a new era of happiness and peace. So, the story goes—again and again—in the great circle of life, which is the grand cycle of awakening.

The more we embrace the laws of awakening, the universal cycle of renewal, the better we become at practicing the noble art of presence. When something emerges in our lives, we should recognize it as a possible teacher and a potential blessing. No tragedy is so great that it cannot lead to something good. No challenge is so big that it cannot become the cause of great discoveries. When something emerges in our mind and psyche, and ultimately in our behavior, we can choose to accept it. In other words: "*When you have shown it, you need to own it.*" This is a great chance for us all. Instead of rejecting and denying, we decide to invite, accept, or at least tolerate it so that we can learn from it. If we can listen to it, it will offer us grounding power. We will extract the light from it and there will be more awareness, more space for conscious presence. Instead of absence, distraction, and struggle, you will have presence—and with this comes the heart and the kindness to be a learner and a sharer.

There is great transforming power in knowing the significance of purpose and its allies: meaning and intention. When you know what you want, life will ultimately find a way to show you how to achieve your goal. The unshakable rock in presence is to have a purpose. It has a meaning and significance and therefore electrifies your intent. Because of this, you will develop stamina, the perseverance to reach your destination. Determination is always aligned with purpose. You know why you are determined, and it helps you to stay on course and find out the how. The Standing Rock Indian Reservation became a news story in 2016 as protests grew against the construction of the Dakota Access Pipeline. The oil pipeline was projected to run through four US states—including the Standing Rock Sioux Reservation, sacred land to the Sioux. The resistance and protests by unarmed Native Americans against an overwhelming authority was a powerful display of human determination. The supremacy of the US Army troops was clear to everyone, but the stamina and non-violent bravery of the protesters carved an image of courage and determination in the minds of millions, making the name Standing Rock a symbol of dignity and empowerment.

We cannot always win, but a great deal can be learned regardless of the outcome. If you are purposeful—aligned with a deep intent—you will gain much from this storehouse, like nurturing rain from a cloud. Intent is in-tension. When you decide to stand by your values and worth, you empower your presence in life. Standing in the center of your being is an affirmation of your sovereignty, uniqueness, and irreplaceable value. Nothing can replace truthfulness to who you are, or the determination to defend and care for all that you hold dear. You may fall and rise many times, but if you are true to yourself, your presence will be felt by others like a peaceful, immovable rock in the river of life.

In Your Land

Having anchored yourself firmly in core values and the identity that is truly you, something immensely significant gradually emerges. Being powerful is not a tight condition or a demonstration of anything.

Empowerment results in a relaxed, peaceful authority. You simply rest in the nature that is you. There is nothing to explain, nothing to defend or justify. There simply is the fact of resting serenely in the center. You are stress-free and aware of being present. This is a highly desired state of consciousness, and often the result of much struggle and learning. And yet it is also the beginning of a new process, as you are discovering something of great depth.

To be firmly rooted in your peaceful power is also to start learning how much you are connected. No true grounding is an isolated focus. We are always part of something, belonging to a greater wholeness. In fact, we always stand deeply connected with the entire world around us. Isolation is an illusion. A magnificent tree is rooted in soil and a part of the land. Its crown receives light and oxygen in the open air and atmosphere. Nothing can thrive in seclusion. We all depend on each other and we are nurtured in the web of connectedness—organically and in consciousness.

Deep connectedness is the truth of all life. When you are standing in your true identity and power, you stand in your land. This land is the land of your accomplishments, your experiences and achievements won through hardships and strenuous efforts. You are never an isolated island. Each and every victory or result is the outcome of countless connections: the schools you attended, the materials you needed, the tools you used, the environments you were part of, the people you exchanged with, the clothes you wore, the food you ate, the air you breathed. So, you are always part of a greater continent, and this vast landmass is part of an even greater mainland, which is part of the Earth that receives energy from the Sun—and on it goes into the infinite connectedness.

As a human being, you are always reliant on other humans. You have grown out of the heredity of your genealogy, generation after generation of relatives, emerging and resulting in your stepping forward into the world. You are connected to your family and the DNA with which you express your nature. You are also associated with the friendships, networks, and local contacts that help define your culture and social identity. There is a great "*we*" wherever there is a clear "*I*." The "*we-ness*" and the "*I-ness*" complement or balance each other. Standing in your land means that you stand in your relationships with your loved ones, your family, friends, and kindred spirits.

Standing in your identity also connects you with the greater nature you are part of. Think about the significance of a garden, a park, or simply the trees, flowers, and grass where you live, the presence of birds, animals, insects, and other sentient life forms. We are immersed into a living sea of life and we affect other beings as they affect us. We are always in landscapes and eco-systems brimming with life. This deep connectedness is what our senses can detect, but we are also immersed into the sea of consciousness, the subtle worlds, or "*second ecology*" as my friend David Spangler calls it. At all levels, we are rooted in the living landscapes and fields of living vibrations.

We are never isolated. We are always part of the greater whole. We belong to wholeness. Anchoring and discovering your ground are a coming home to yourself and your deep connectedness with all sentient life. This potentially gives you tremendous power as you draw on the storehouse of your greater fullness. You gain access to the larger lands you are part of, and you gain the authentic right to claim resources from these vast realities as they also receive from you. The law of reciprocity, mutuality, and continued exchange is always at work. In reality, it is the great breath of life, the incoming and outgoing wave of life in movement.

○ GIFT ○
Simply Stand

Here is a short and natural exercise you can try. It is so simple, and yet it can be very deep when you invest your presence in it and try it more than once.

Give yourself the experience of simply standing in your presence. Stand up and feel relaxed. Close your eyes. Let go of tensions in your muscles. Just stand and feel the weight of your body. Feel how you balance in your standing. Sense the warmth, and perhaps if you are somewhat cold, sense that too. Relax and let your breath extend to the whole body. Feel how your whole body is one wholeness, one organism, alive, vibrating, pulsating.

Now, let your attention expand into your emotional presence. Be aware of your feelings and allow them to relax. Let the physical relaxation become emotional peacefulness, a simple resting in being present and awake. Sense the atmosphere within you. Allow calmness to be present. Allow yourself to be part of stillness, and sense how it feels to stand, upright and balanced.

Let your attention expand into your mind. Recognize your thoughts as part of your inner world, and allow them to settle down, or to become aware of the relaxed position. Focus on the simple fact that you stand. Realize that in standing, you stand out. You stand out and you stand by. You are standing up in the landscape. You have arisen. You have emerged. You are right where you are, resting in yourself.

Realize that while standing, you are in the center of your being, and you are valuable in your uniqueness. You are irreplaceable, standing in your sovereignty. Honor yourself as an expression of universal life. Honor yourself as part of nature. Honor yourself as a human being. Honor yourself as an inimitable identity, making a real difference, contributing to the entirety of life.

When it feels right, gently open your eyes and sense your surroundings. Connect with everything around you. Effortlessly, you are anchored in your being and connected to the greater world, part of the great flow of life. Return to your activities with a renewed sense of being present and awake.

6

THE FLOW DANCER

Learning the art of walking took you to many places,
Discovering a multitude of weird and distant realms,
But also exhausting your weary feet.
One day you heard the word "dance,"
And the world became a poem.

Flow or No-Go

Life is a dangerous and wonderful adventure. If you have no compass, you probably end up as driftwood tossed around on a stormy ocean. Without a doubt, there is great learning in the world of ever-changing waves, taking you to places you never dreamt of or believed possible. Being a traveler on a journey of ups and downs offers a wealth of experiences, hopes and disappointments, anticipations and victories, surprises and trivialities—the entire curriculum of culture and skills that gradually educate you to stand on your own feet.

When you feel that confidence and self-reliance have, to a certain extent, landed in the soil of your life, and you have accomplished basic success in the jungle of achievements, a new phase of learning becomes relevant. As a solid standing stone in the landscape of your world, open the gateway to the realm of subtle and gracious movements. Living your life constantly involves entering unchartered territory. If you truly want to be good at navigating your course, it is of the upmost importance that you open your outer and inner ears to listen. What do you pick up? Which signals to you register? Does your head say *"yes"* with great conviction whereas your stomach tightens slightly? Do you see a desired path ahead, yet sense other possible routes that could bring you to the goal? Do you block certain sensations and try to focus on the anticipated?

Tuning Fork

You need to become your own tuning fork and to stay true to what you sense. Is it real or false? Is it transient or lasting? Is it helpful or does it create inhibition and handicaps? Be alert and interested in catching the most fleeting impulses. First signals are often almost undetectable, incredibly fragile and delicate, and easy to ignore. However, if you want to live life not only as anchored or solid stone, but also with the fluidity and grace that makes miracles happen, you must learn the subtle art of deep flow. Usually, there is a split within us between different parts of our nature, making flow certainly very difficult, if not unlikely. When you are absent-minded, it is difficult to act with authenticity. You want to do the right thing but are distracted by memories and emotional reactions. You strive to perform but are haunted by other people's expectations of you. You are really bored by what you do and yet you need to be brilliant in order to have success. You are stubborn and will not let go of old behavior patterns, until everything comes crashing down around you. We all recognize these typical situations—and they are far from being any kind of flow.

"Intent-Presence"

The challenge is that when you are separated into different, opposing parts, you become alienated from yourself. You end up being a house divided against itself in which nothing really works. Intention must be aligned with presence. This is a big thing. It is also very important if you are ultimately to become a dancer in life. So, what does flow require? Not just flow on the surface, but deep flow. You need to be passionately present and undivided in your engagement. There can be no reservations or emotional stumbling blocks. If you become too excited or try to be in control, you will probably drop out of the wave of flow. The flow zone is between anxiety, fear, or control on the one hand and boredom, sleepiness, or over-relaxedness on the other. It is a naturally relaxed tension of deep interest. The flow zone opens when you are joyfully engaged, fully present, and open to what is happening. In other words, you are undivided and your activities, in a way, become effortless because you accept the fluidity of the moment. Heart and mind work as one and the body becomes their living expression. There is no internal conflict, no analyzing process opposed to emotional reactions.

Act or Not—and Learn

On the other hand, you should recognize when not to act. If your tuning fork tells you to step back and reflect, do not ignore it. Take it seriously. There may be "unfinished business" within you, and you may need to address these previously unnoticed parts of you before you more forward. But it may also be that things are simply not right for you. Perhaps you cannot rationalize it instantly and explain why, but whatever it is will eventually emerge. For the time being, you probably just need to be true to your gut feeling and hold back. It is important to exercise this "early" or "instant" sensing, for it will make you more skilled in listening and learning. Mistakes in learning are inevitable—which makes them really valuable. They help you to follow your compass needle without distractions. In order to hit the bull's-eye, we need to learn that missing the point is part of the calibrating process. You can only learn through failure. In fact, success is the product of failures.

There Will Be Performers

Flow is all about freedom. When you are divided, you are not free. It is both very simple and extremely complex. When you have an open heart, a flexible mind, and emotional willingness, things will smoothly transform from being to doing. This is soul-body flow, resulting in more power, more love, and more creativity. You are a conduit for unimpeded life flow. But how on earth can this be accomplished? It can only happen if you invite everything within you to engage in a completely new co-operative relationship. It is a big story but can in essence briefly be shared.

Regard yourself as a theater stage in the world. You are here to perform plays that have never been expressed before. You are a storyteller, director, and performer at the same time. In fact, you are the entire playhouse, and all the parts within you are needed for the stories to be played out on the stage. Your inner author is the spiritual fountain at the core of your being—the source of the desire to tell the stories you will perform. You are here to tell stories that are

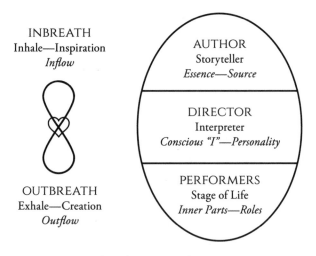

INBREATH
Inhale—Inspiration
Inflow

OUTBREATH
Exhale—Creation
Outflow

AUTHOR
Storyteller
Essence—Source

DIRECTOR
Interpreter
Conscious "I"—Personality

PERFORMERS
Stage of Life
Inner Parts—Roles

What do you perform?
Who are your players on the scene?
What is your story?

unique and new to the world. Not copies or repetitions—always original dramas. Your inner director is your conscious ability to give a personal interpretation of the story, a distinctive touch, and a flavor that will never be repeated. Finally, your inner performers are all the roles and talents you have at your disposal in your conscious and subconscious nature. These parts within you are the means to express and unfold the full story. They are the dancers and players. Your task is to initiate and manifest the cooperative effort that brings the story onto the stage.

Just think about this amazing perspective. All the parts within you are invited to participate equally with their own moves, their own qualities, their own dance on the stage of life. Doesn't it sound wonderful to invite this to happen? You may ask whether it is in any way possible. How can I bring the conflicting parts together into a real collaborative effort? The answer lies in a few simple but fundamental facts:

I. Invite and greet each part of your inner life (such as roles, voices, sub-personalities, aspects, living parts, conditions) with sincere interest.

II. Encounter each part of your inner life with the same respect you would show another individual or fellow human being.

III. Make space for any part of your inner life: listen and let it be heard and respected where it is, and never try to fix, cheat, lecture, or outsmart it.

IV. Offer to become a friend to each part of your inner life, to be a partner in freedom and according to need.

It works. Once a suitable framework has been made and simple guidelines are followed, any part of your inner life will respond and eventually cooperate with you and transform into its core nature, namely intelligent, kind, and powerful. I can only repeat: It works. The psychology is exactly the same as when we meet other people.

If they accept an open invitation and are met with hospitality and appreciation of their uniqueness, sooner or later they will want to join the crew of dancers on your stage of life. There are good reasons for their dysfunctional behavior. When they sense that they are being shown respect, patience, and sincere interest, they will want to be part of the team of performers, their deepest abilities will start to unfold, and their rich diversity will blossom. An anxious and nervous part may conceal a caring and gentle nature, a sly and cunning part may contain a bright intelligence, and an angry or hating part perhaps holds great authority and power—and so on.

You need to gather your crew so that you can perform the plays of your inner storyteller, as interpreted by the director within you. What are these plays? They are the authentic way you do whatever you do. It may be as a skillful carpenter, a parent or professional teacher, a genuine friend, a good neighbor, or simply a unique human being with a broad spectrum of qualities and features. You have your own compass needle and your own core values to find your way through the world and be creative. You need to be you and no one else. Comparing is toxic to authenticity. *The real deal is what you feel.* Stay true to your special way of being you, appreciate the space you fill out, and connect with others in the same spirit. There will be plenty of things to do. The way you encounter your own inner crew of performers and assemble them to dance will be reflected in the way you engage with other people.

We all have conditioned parts in our subconscious. They are like prisoners trapped in a time warp in the past, no longer relating to the present but reacting with strategies they believe will work. These inner parts of ours cause us headaches, stress, performance anxiety, loss of energy, inertia, to withhold emotions, have outbursts of frustration, and to resist simply being. These convicts all possess the most wonderful capabilities, but we need to release them. We need to understand that our greatest inner adversaries truly are our potentially most trusted allies. When we are ready to meet them, something remarkable will start to unfold. It is somewhat like the film *Inside Out*, where *"the little voices inside the head"* learn to cooperate. You and I can gather our crew of performers. This is where the dance begins in our life. Inspirations are freely formulated in understandable ways, and there is emotional support—free passage. The result is creative activity, with humor and acceptance, but also tested and trained to grow and mature.

Primal Ritual

It is late August in 2016 and my dear friend Kenneth is getting married to his Norwegian partner Karianne. I have the great honor and joy to be his best man. The wedding is being held in Holmenkollen, north of Oslo. It is a fantastic and bountiful event, and everything emanates love and generosity. At the dinner after the ceremony, my speech is about being a man in conscious, evolutionary growth and I honor my friend as a marvelous role model.

Later the same evening, there is dancing in the old restaurant. Kenneth and I throw ourselves into a wild stunt on the dance floor, expressing the joy and energy we have felt so often with the students in our SoulFlow workshops. Now he is a stylish and graceful groom in a classy suit, the spitting image of masculine elegance in movement. I sense that I am liberated in a deep way right there on the wooden floor. The other guests are hurling themselves around in a boisterously festive manner. Of course, our male tribal dance is surpassed by Kenneth and Karianne's bridal waltz. Later. it seems that almost everybody is on the dance floor.

In a strange but very natural way, I feel extremely free and in a good and open mood. Something is different, as if a part of me is letting itself loose from within—and I do not resist it. At a certain point, I discover that one of my female dance partners, a beautiful young woman, doesn't want our dance to stop. I don't give it a second thought but continue the sweaty show. It is sheer bodily delight in rhythmic expression, and a pleasure to unfold on a dance floor with a person I do not know. There is something raw and native about it, but at the same time, it feels like a refined unfoldment of flow.

I am in pure enjoyment. I don't feel any personal attraction to my dance partner, but there is a primal power present and I am part of it. It is in the dance itself, in the pulse, and in the presence of this primeval pair. It is an almost timeless manifestation, right there in that wooden building in Norway.

Even though I do not realize it in the moment, something profound and strong has been let loose. I can only witness it. I am still a happily married man and I neither flirt nor imagine being with any women other than my wife and partner of the past thirty years. Nevertheless, something is beginning to happen, and it will take me time to decipher what it means. The haunting words from W.B. Yeats's play *The Land of Heart's Desire* captures the essence of my feelings:

> "Faeries, come take me out of this dull world,
> For I would ride with you upon the wind,
> Run on the top of the dishevelled tide,
> And dance upon the mountains like a flame!"

I do not live a boring life, but something deep down is moving. I often think how good it is not to know what life has in store for us. How utterly demotivating, and scary too, the world would be if we had a detailed precognition of future events—with no surprises. We may have a clear sense of purpose and direction in life—which I have been fortunate enough to experience most of all my life—but I still think it is a blessing not to be burdened in advance with details of the journey and how we will reach the many staging posts. Looking back, I was almost like a boy who would soon be thrown clueless into the storms of maturation. The wedding in Holmenkollen was like a sweet oasis before the tempest broke.

Inviting the Unknown

The nature of the dancer lies hidden in every moment of the unfolding. It is not confined by habits and conventions, expectations and planning. Customary, habitual life is crammed with routines and well-known pathways. In many ways, we can live a normal life with an absent mind, immersed in daydreaming while we automatically perform our "formalities of saneness." The dancer is not in sight. We will catch only a faint trace of this elusive presence in the scent of our dreamy longings.

We could say that it is only when we get so fed up and disappointed with daily living and duties that we are in effect almost pushed out of the box for an instant. In a moment of unexpected bewilderment, we experience a new opening to the present. What opens in the gap between then and now might be alarmingly confusing, unusually threatening, or outrageously beautiful. Either way, it is the fresh breath of newness, and a possible invitation into the unknown. Why should we leave the world we know and accept an invitation into the unknown, with no guarantees of anything good? Perhaps the answer is that life is never just what we anticipate, that we can never control the wildness of spirit.

Becoming the dancer is to say "*yes*" to the unknown, but it is also to listen to the deep call in the wind, the call of innocence and untamed presence. So, in a way, the unknown is not entirely unfamiliar. It is like a peculiar, albeit meaningful memory of things forgotten. It is a stirring of the free, spontaneous playfulness we all keep in the center of our being, but too often hold down and struggle to ignore. The rousing of strange rhythms on a wooden floor at a wedding, a split second of fragile beauty when a raindrop gathers under a petal in a gentle shower, or the weird waves of tenderness rippling through you when you look into the eyes of another human being—all this and more may be the tiny portal into the forgotten world of marvels.

For this to happen, we need to recognize the risky nature of life and accept that we are never in control of everything. We cannot control death, the weather, our encounters with others, challenges, circumstances, or blessings. The control panel of the brain is highly skilled in a multitude of functions, such as calculating, remembering, analyzing, comparing, discerning, categorizing, and verbalizing.

The brain, however, is not the sum total of our being, and while it deserves credit for its myriad capabilities, we should also give credit to the many levels of human functionality—such as our will, instincts, feelings, imagination, and intuition, to name just a few.

Becoming a dancer in your life is to invite joy and spontaneity to become dance partners. From this come moments of unexpected creativity, periods of effortless buoyancy, and windows of blessed opportunities. But you must be willing to take risks rather than just talk endlessly about probabilities, calculated outcomes, and possible losses. You have to step into the river and taste the water. This is the testing ground for having faith in life. Do you genuinely believe that life will support you if you trust that doing your best—truthfully and with a gentle heart—is the way ahead? Daring implies that unforeseen dangers and challenges will present themselves. That is part of becoming a surfer on the waves of the great breath of life. When you act with courage and trust, you will undoubtedly encounter failures, but you will also evolve your inner radar and the ability to use your tuning fork and avoid mistakes as you follow your heart's direction. Here are a few guidelines on your journey into unknown territory, where dancers are born, and the world becomes a poem:

If One Thing Is Certain, It Is That Nothing Is Certain

Lean into this and trust that life is beneficial. If you dare to follow your heart, you will be supported by the starry sky and the green earth. *Life is not a pre-planned marketing strategy to follow, but a mystery to unravel*—nothing can be guaranteed beforehand, but everything holds possible blessings.

Root Yourself and Drink Nectar

Connect with your anchored awareness and remember that you are always a standing stone in the landscape of your life. Then, open yourself up to delight and let it seduce you. When you are rooted in "being you," there are innumerable gifts of joy to discover as you stay true to yourself and follow your dream.

Get Lost and Find Your Way

Do something new that will take you out on a limb. Look to the side where you usually do not focus. The openings are often inches away from where you stare. You are not blindfolded but life shapeshifts in front of you and you discover new pathways where you didn't imagine it possible. As a dancing treasure-hunter, you become the friend of undiscovered places, staring right at you.

Follow Inspiration No Matter Where It Leads You

Never set conditions to inspiration. Surrender and let it shock you with surprises of wonder and amazement that will shake and change you. *Inspiration is not an agenda; it is a wild thing.* If you hold back and overanalyze, it will fly away, probably without trace, like a rare butterfly. Inspiration, from the Latin *"inspirare"* (to breathe life, or spirit, into), is born in wildness—so be wild with it!

Straight Paths Are Winding, and the Shortest Is the Circle

The art of dancing is to learn to surf with what already exists. The interesting features on the path from A to B are always where you happen to be, not where you came from or hope to be next. Everything moves in circles of renewal, breathing in, pausing, breathing out, pausing, being in the moment of the now.

The Untamed Self Is Barefoot

"Life always finds a way"—so the saying goes—and our bountiful planet is a good example of this. On your way through life, remember to take your shoes off now and again to allow your feet to make direct contact with the earth that supports you, your foundation. Make it a regular exercise to stand barefoot in the grass or on the soil. You may be surprised by what comes of it, and even find yourself dancing.

You Have Access to Everything—When There Is Attunement

As a dancer in life, you will see doors open and allow you to visit places where few—if any—others have been. It is all about attunement.

Access is granted where there is compatibility in vibration, as equal attracts equal. It is the living flow in you that brings you to previously secret destinations. Life comes to meet you when you are ready and it carries you along.

○ Gift ○
Breathe with Gentleness

Give yourself the gift of a peaceful moment. This simple exercise takes only a few minutes but can last longer if you like it. There is a short version and a longer version—you decide.

Sit comfortably, give yourself a moment to experience how you relax, and let go of possible tensions in your body. Pay attention to your stomach and relax. Pay attention to your head and neck and relax. Feel your whole body as a living world—supporting you so that you can live your life. Let your whole body relax.

Let your relaxation extend to your emotional state. Sense how you allow yourself to experience a quietness in your emotional atmosphere. Like small feathers or snowflakes silently descending and landing on the ground, let your inner environment feel a softness and a calm for a moment.

Allow your thoughts to be within you, but do not follow them. Look at them for a moment as living entities in your inner landscape, or as clouds in the sky. Accept them, but stay a quiet observer, a peaceful witness.

Then be aware of your breathing. Sense how your breath is a gentle, pulsating wave on the shore of your life. If you need to do so, take a deep breath, then leave it to its own rhythm. Sense how it connects to your whole body and is not just something in your chest. Sense its softness. Sense how it is both very subtle and very powerful in its gentleness.

Experience being able to witness that there is a kindness in the way you breathe. There is a tenderness in your breath, a mildness—so simple, so beautiful.

Breathe gently, and let the waves be a felt appreciation towards your whole body. Let your body be immersed in a gratefulness for the body and its constant activity. Embrace your body with your kind, gentle breath.

Breathe gently, and let the waves be a felt appreciation towards your emotional life. Let your inner ambience, or state of mind, be immersed in a gratefulness for emotions and the learning they make possible. Embrace your emotional life with your kind, gentle breath.

Breathe gently, and let the waves be a felt appreciation towards your mental life. Let the nature of your thought be immersed in a gratefulness for the mind and its manifold skills. Embrace your mind with your kind, gentle breath.

Breathe gently, and let the waves be a felt appreciation towards your personality. Let your personal identity be immersed in a gratefulness for the conscious "I" and its role in your life. Embrace your personality with your kind, gentle breath.

Breathe gently, and let the waves be a felt appreciation towards your life and relations. Let your life and relations be immersed in a gratefulness for the journey of your life and what it unfolds. Embrace your life journey with your kind, gentle breath.

You can extend the gentle breath to nature, to other people or beings, or to the entire world. You can also simply stay with the beauty and grace of breathing with kindness, letting a warmth be felt from your breast like a warm sun radiating gentleness through your whole inner and outer nature.

When it feels natural, simply open your eyes, move your body, and return to your activities with a touch of gentleness and a somewhat more relaxed breath.

7

THE FIREDREAMER

The old, experienced, and sharp thought approached,
And addressed imagination with slightly suspicious eyes:
"Hey there, restless, strange nomad,
Why are you so colorfully dressed?"
Imagination looked back with a warm and gentle smile:
"Hi, friend, you look at the color of my skin."

You Can Never Figure It Out

Life is overwhelmingly surprising. No matter how fast your mind works, it can never calculate all the factors in a given situation. If you try to analyze and intellectually understand the given angles in anything, you will arrive too late at the station and miss the train of life. You cannot anticipate unforeseen circumstances. The weather may change. A person may arrive late. You may catch the flu. You are in dire trouble if you invest all your energy in the smartness of the mind.

Let me use another image. You own an entire house with several floors and many rooms. Living on one of the floors and in one of the rooms is an efficient calculator, a scrutinizing, thinking resident. This inhabitant is just one of many dwellers in the large house, yet all the other tenants seem to have handed over their keys, bank accounts, and passwords to this sole occupant, when they are in fact supposed to be a cooperative fellowship of the house. This position cannot show the way ahead. No matter how smart you try to be, you cannot sit in the ivory tower of your mind and figure things out from there. You will end up losing all the things you hold dear.

Ponder this for a moment. Our practical skills have given us the chemical know-how we use in many marvelous ways, but also a ruthlessly profit-oriented pharmaceutical industry. Technologically, we have developed various beneficial means of transportation, but also a cynical, high-tech arms industry. We have created the means to live pleasant lives without hunger and many diseases, but also slums, drug dealers, and desperate starvation. Driven by unrealized manipulative greed and fear, the rational mind has created toxic, planetary pollution, unfair, worldwide discrimination, global poverty, and countless wars. Left to its own devices, the rational mind ends up as a puppet of unrealized powers who sorely needs to partner with its siblings. As a team serving the greater good, they can do incredibly good things, but alone and isolated, they crash and fail through being one-sided.

Accept that your mind is a great part of you, a wonderful interpreter, a great form builder, an impressive ally in practical solutions, but at the same time a depraved and incompetent dictator that will never succeed if elected supreme leader. Hidden agendas and unrealized motivations will outsmart it. In fact, this has long been the case. It is the archetypal story of the sorcerer's apprentice who lets loose powers that then run wild.

Imagination Is Real

"Are you sure it is not just something you imagined?" Who has not heard this "sobering" voice of so-called sanity? Let it be very clear that we are indeed able to perceive things that are figments of our

inner imbalances, fears, prejudices, and self-limiting convictions. Having said that, we need to reconsider what we mean by imagination. Look around you. If you are in a building, everything around you is "*just something imagined*" that has manifested itself. The walls, floor, roof, furniture—yes, everything defining the room you are in is externalized imagination. Even the clothes you wear, the way you wear them—and your hairstyle—are all "*just something imagined.*" Yes—imagined and expressed. Even the most unstable and fluctuating images and feelings you contain have their own reality and affect your health and life. It is not "just" something. It is definitely something!

In our present world, we normally take intellect as the measuring stick for everything else. We do so because of the success of the practical, operational mind that has created computers, machines, instruments, devices, and tools. We have been well served by the rational mind. It has increased our life quality, ways of survival, and practical living, and this is no mean achievement. It's actually a big deal. Nevertheless, we have become prisoners of our liberating assistant. Today, we must battle to maintain the significance and importance of the heart, light, and power of our greater presence. We have sacrificed almost everything on the altar of operational rationality. One could ask where this leaves sensitivity, empathy, unspoiled passion, and innocent imagination in ruling world affairs? They have ended up as passengers in the efficient vehicle of the rational, practical, result-oriented mind. However, these passengers are prominent powers in themselves and we should assign them equal status. In fact, the only hope for the world lies in inviting them onto the stage to assist the poor, overloaded, and hyper-busy intellect that cannot by itself solve the problems created.

Imagination is real. It is intimately connected with feelings, passion, and sensitivity, along with curiosity, perception, and the inventive spirit. Imagination provides the wings we need to fly to unrealized destinations. Mind and heart can meet and join efforts on the wings of our imaginative Pegasus as we soar and fly.

Allow!

Understanding the secrets of imagination is an amazing journey. Our imaginative powers are very different from pure feelings and thoughts, yet they contain both as a sensitive and perceptive presence. Imagination is intimately connected with allowing for perception and keeping a flexible focus simultaneously. The ability to allow sounds easier than it is. Mostly, we operate with a rather strict intellectual and emotional filter that allows only fairly well-known and anticipated impressions in order to gain access to our daily consciousness. We need to learn to give a huge green light to a new journey. Check it out for yourself. Does any of this sound familiar to you?

What is the purpose of this?
It's unattainable!
It's illogical!
I feel this is too huge!
It's completely naïve!
This cannot be for real!
I do not deserve this!
Which verifiable data makes this credible?
This is pure fantasy!

Consider these and similar "bodyguards" of the rational mind to be the protectors of the status quo and think for a moment how likely it is that completely new impressions will be able to get pass them. No wonder inventive solutions and revolutionary ideas often have an incredibly hard time entering our physical world. So, what are your typical objections? What do your bodyguards against imaginative renewal look like?

How do we do it? How do you and I find a way to accept imagination as a strong and loved partner on our journey of awakening? There are many ways, but here are some suggestions you may appreciate and wish to investigate:

Give Your Felt Permission

First, invite yourself to explore the amazing world of imagination. This is like signing up for an adventure. You unlock the doors of inner perception by giving it a green light, not just in your mind, but also in your emotional nature. You must feel a "*yes*"—a longing to discover new continents within you without preconditions. The mind itself cannot decipher the password to an open-minded exploration. You need to connect with your emotional yearning, the desire to become more alive and open. You need to feel how it is to give a "*yes*." This may take some time, but it starts with determination. Be clear in your mind and stretch out your hands to your sensitive nature and—if possible—to your instinctual urge for passionate presence. In other words, give yourself permission to embark on the journey. Be prepared to meet opposition to this foolish suggestion. A crowd of suspicious voices may come together and try to persuade you to come to your senses since you have obviously lost your marbles.

Be Breezily Playful

As a child, you were open to wonder, with no definitions and conventions of any kind in your head. Gradually, you became entangled by the countless rules and regulations of adult life, and probably lost some of the magical connection to wonder. Now it is time to reconnect with the innocent nature of being fully present, to look at raindrops running down a window, to let your associations run free while you enjoy the scent of something, or to dance to music when you feel a tingling sensation in your body. Perhaps you need to lose your way in order to find a new path. Being playful has many faces. Some of it is reflected in your body, where you move and how you move. Watch children and how they handle their bodies. Do you need to relearn any of this? Then there is the inner part of playfulness. Either-or, is never enough. So where does the path between them lead you? Have you tried to join the opposites? Think about how much space there is between East and West, North and South!

Ask with Gentle Passion

In the fantasy adventure film, *The Golden Compass*, a wise old man says at one point: *"Hold the question in your mind, but lightly, like it was something alive."* This is a wonderful guideline for the creative imagination. Be gentle in your curiosity and treat the question as a living creature. The approach itself is imaginative. You might even ask yourself what your question looks like, or what color, shape, taste, smell, and feeling it has—for there is a profound wisdom in the notion that the question is the answer. Let it test you and challenge you. The way you ask determines the way the answer comes and the nature of the answer. The noble art of asking is precious. We so often strangle the answer by our choking way of asking. Ask with gentle passion. Ask with tender care. Have you tried it? Really tried? Try again!

Trust Your Untainted Impressions

We so often cancel important impressions by letting them come up against our bodyguards of rationality. Or we overreact emotionally and blow them out of proportion, distorting their core nature. Let impressions do their work on you without dismissing them. Trust your impressions. Do not add, do not subtract. Let them stimulate you and invite you. It is normal to exaggerate things and make them bigger than they are, but we also try to diminish anything that inconveniences our behavior and traditions. How about giving impressions a chance on their own? Simply register them and let them guide you in a new direction. Everything tells a story. What is your impression telling you? Listen carefully. It may be a good idea to dare to try something totally new. Perhaps you should wait and just listen? The impression might lead you if you trust it.

How I Discovered "What If ..."

I will share some personal experiences with you. You may recognize some of them from your own life, and parts of them will perhaps challenge you. It's all very natural, even basic, yet full of wonder when it happens.

The Future Presence

In 2007, I was sitting in an airplane with my friend and colleague Kenneth on a flight returning from California to Denmark. We had just attended a spiritual conference as guest teachers. Because it had been a great success, we were invited back several times by Michael D. Robbins, founder of The Seven Ray Institute. We both felt uplifted. The sun was shining, and in the bright cabin, we were taking in the impressions and experiencing a sense of gratitude that our presentations had been so wonderfully received by the many participants and, not least, by our international colleagues. As the plane took off, Kenneth suddenly asked me: "*Søren, what will your work be like ten years from now?*" I was a little surprised, and my head was a little tired, so a part of me didn't want to play along. However, there was a relevance to his question as this trip felt like a very important beginning of something new. I had just met David Spangler and his wife, Julia, for the first time. David had also been invited to the conference as a teacher. I had heard him speak live and we had a long conversation the morning after. So, Kenneth's question made sense, coming as it did after this significant journey.

I leaned back in my seat, looked out the window, and imagined myself ten years from now. Within seconds, I felt a warm, golden glow, as if I had already moved forward in linear time and reached a room in the future present. My response to Kenneth was that in ten years' time I would be working much more deeply with people in personal sessions, and with experimental workshops where sharing experiences would be as important as teaching. I had a distinct feeling of psychological depth and intimacy, and of wisdom emerging out of presence, in an atmosphere tinged with a golden "flavor." Two years later, I started taking clients, giving fewer lectures as workshops became much more in-depth, and today I recognize that what I sensed and what inspired my imagination in that moment is now a living reality.

Something in me already knew and sensed what lay ahead. Had I not trusted my impressions as I flew out of LA on that sunny day, I don't think I would have any recollection of that specific flight at all. Today, it is a clear memory with an intense, condensed atmosphere.

The Vow That Was Changed

In 2011, I was taught and trained in the method that Kenneth and I went on to develop into what today is called the SoulFlow Method. My excellent teacher was Gordon Davidson, an American colleague with deep and wise skills in approaching and helping the suffering inner parts—sometimes called subpersonalities—we have in our inner psyche and mind. In my case, the topic was lack of finances. The session began with a guided meditation, followed by an invitation to the parts within me that lived in a situation of shortage. I opened myself to this atmosphere of insufficiency and was astonished to see, with my inner eye, a monk clad in robes. He was very convinced that vowing to live in poverty and serve Christ was the way ahead. Gordon suggested I ask the monk to share. The monk told me that he had done this for ages, that this was the way to serve God. He lived for this abundance in Christ.

Gordon also suggested I ask the monk if he felt his world was now rich and full of abundance. The monk was surprised by the question and I sensed how he perceived his once abundant world as a dry desert today. He was loyal to an ancient oath. He persevered. He served! However, it was weary work now, much harder than before. Gordon next asked me if there were other figures present with similar convictions. Almost before he had finished his question, I sensed the presence of more monks, a priest or bishop in ornamented robes, and an Indian sannyasi in orange saffron robes. They had somehow gathered in the same space as kindred spirits who share a similar belief. The bishop was impressive, but his attire was not his own; it belonged to the church. They had sworn an oath to serve a divine being and to renounce all belongings. They were profoundly sincere and loyal, but their present world resembled an arid wilderness.

At Gordon's prompting, I proposed to them all that perhaps the time had come to let go of their ancient pledges and make a new vow. To my surprise, they collectively agreed to do so. With Gordon's help, I asked them to revoke their pledges and to affirm a new oath of abundance in all its facets, accepting that money was a magnificent way to serve God, Christ, and the Divine in all manner of ways. I subsequently witnessed how the group of inner servants stepped across the threshold into a new space of radiant, fertile abundance and joy. It was extremely liberating, and I felt as if a heavy burden had been lifted from my shoulders.

But the story does not end here. The important, culminating event came just weeks later when I held my next workshop. The income from this single event was greater than anything I had done before, and it changed my financial situation. Meeting the inner sub-personalities with a deeply felt sense of empathy and offering them a "new deal" was a crucial turning point in my professional life. It was a valuable learning experience that inner convictions can be transformed if they are met with warm understanding and offered new expression—all made possible by trusting their "imaginative presence," not just as fantasies, but also as living inner parts. The key point had been: What if we try something completely new?

A Book That Was Already There
In 2012, my friend and publisher at Lemuel Books, Kirsten Puggaard, wanted to hold an event about angels and she asked me if I would like to participate and also write something about angels that could be sold at the event. I said yes but was unsure about the writing part. My huge, almost 800-page Danish book *Levende Visdom (Living Wisdom)*, published in 2008, had a long chapter on the subject, but it would need to be taken out as a kind of article for the event. Somehow it didn't feel right. Kirsten then mentioned another book I had written and asked whether I could extend it to include more about angels, but we realized that would not be practically possible. She then casually suggested: "*Well, you could just write a new book*

about angels and I could publish it for the event?" I smiled back at her and responded: *"Wow, that would be great, but I don't have the time right now for such a project."*

We said goodbye and I took a walk to catch the bus home. However, the funny thing was that even before I got into the bus, a fully developed idea was maturing within me, as if it had been there for some time. In my mind, I saw a complete book, not about the angels around us, but the mostly suppressed angelic qualities we all have within us. I was optimistic that it would require little or no effort to write. All I would simply have to do was "lean into" the inspirational atmosphere and let it guide me. My rational mind was struggling as I had so much work to do and the idea of writing a new book seemed silly and unrealistic, and the timing completely wrong.

Three weeks later, I handed the finished manuscript of *The Angel Within You* to Kirsten and the book was published soon after. The writing process was a completely new journey, full of liberated inspiration, and it became the first of my recent "flowbooks," created almost effortlessly in an entirely new way. The book ended up selling quite well and is still a cornerstone in my writing career. In fact, Denmark's biggest publishers made a deal with Kirsten's tiny company and ended up selling the book via their book club. By the way, Kirsten did organize other great events, but the one about angels never came to fruition. The process illustrated very clearly to me that even if my rational mind has many opinions and frames set up, a hugely creative process could still be stirring at a deeper level, awaiting the opportunity to erupt. Thanks to Kirsten's "casual" suggestion, something immensely important emerged in my life as a writer and author.

An Unexpected Invitation

In November 2013, I was conducting a workshop about SidheWisdom, or Wild Spirituality, in Denmark's Northern Jutland region. It was Saturday evening and our first day of teaching had ended. It had been a good day and I was feeling quietly cheerful. Upstairs in the room where I was sleeping, the atmosphere was fresh, as if a breeze had just blown through the place. Suddenly, I had an urge to sit with my back against the wall and meditate. I put pen and paper next to me in case I felt inspired to write down something. Sitting cross-legged with my spine straight but relaxed, I opened myself to the freshness of the presence, not only in the room, but also inside me. My mind was clear and open, and I sensed a cool brightness and clarity.

Focusing on the theme of Wild Spirituality as I "leaned into" the atmosphere, I gradually became conscious of a distinct, living presence within me, as if someone was approaching. It was a dignified presence, very erect and individual, as if a person was addressing me—a physical person with distinct features, but with nature playing the greater part of the whole. I also felt the presence of rocks and forests and a northern tone in the approaching individual, a male who took the opportunity to share some condensed thoughts or images with me. Keeping my focus, I picked up the paper and wrote down what came from him straight to my mind:

"Our musicality comes from the fact that we listen with full attention to the notes of living beings and everything around us. The sounds dance on the background of silence. We listen to the language of sounds—the music of wholeness. The music of the earth and the mountains. The music of the water and the rain. The music of the air and the wind. The music of the sun and the fire. The crises and conflicts of human life hurt our ears. We are more inclined to withdraw. We have to overcome this inclination in order to stay. Humans think in separated words—as speech. We think in coherent verses—like music. Humans often act in separating ways. We act in combining ways like tunes in a song. Begin to think more musically. Melodious—tuneful. Learn to feel through connections—tonally. Try to act more organically, kindly, vibrantly."

That was it. The atmosphere was permeated with fir trees, rocks, and the smell of moss and heather. I felt I was in the company of a kind, kindred spirit who was interested in exchange and who had stated a position and encouraged me to embark on a new journey. I gradually came back to my outer activity and read what I had written down. It felt fresh, as if the wind from the wilderness had blown gently through the room. Then the daily mind took over again: What should I do with this? Was my mind playing games? Was I drowning in a kind of wishful thinking, believing that I was now in contact with elves, like those in the world of Tolkien?

This was the beginning of a completely new exploration in the succeeding years. I had to stand by my clear impressions and neither exaggerate nor ignore them. I decided to follow up on the encounter and to remain true to the benign new friend, no matter how the surrounding world reacted. I had to summon up the courage to deal with those reactions anticipated, for I knew it would be a tricky venture to claim that faeries, elves or Sidhe are in fact living realities close to our realm. The encounter further unfolded in learning about how we can discover amazing yet entirely natural things when our minds are ready. I started to learn practically, not just in theory, that reality is much more multi-dimensional than our brains are trained to relate to. I opened to "*what if.*"

What if you just wrote a book? What if you went forward ten years? What if you changed your vow of abundance? What if you were approached by a Sidhe?

Are you ready to be surprised? How far will you go? What holds you back from stepping into unexpected terrain? Do you dare to ride your dragon of imagination and find out where it leads you? Inviting your inner FireDreamer may turn out to be more real than you ever dreamt of.

Fiery Hope

It's all in the mind. The way we perceive things determines their destiny. This is true of hope as well. To many people, hope includes a degree of wishful thinking. When a person says: "*Oh, I really hope it will be possible sometime in the future,*" he may be expressing hope, but his rational mind is thinking along entirely different lines. Hope thus becomes associated with a certain sadness or lack of something, possibly even great uncertainty and fear. But fear and pure hope are not linked.

Let's turn it around: *"Hope springs eternal in the human breast."* These words by Alexander Pope remind us that we have an irrepressible, constantly renewing force within us. Hope is the opposite of despair, disillusion, and resignation. At its core, hope is born not from a lack of energy—quite the opposite. Real hope is a power connected with a knowing and a vision about what is possible and what can manifest. This hope is having confidence in the possible, in the support life will give, and in what is in the making. My friend David Spangler has said that hope is the place where opportunities go to be born. This makes hope the antidote to the poison of despair. It becomes a living power linked with vision and a determination to try things out, to open doors instead of closing them. The creative imagination is nurtured, and the perceptive powers are fully invested in engaging with possible ways ahead.

No new impulses can emerge if we lock "factuality" into any given framework. We end up paralyzed in the unchangeable grip of so-called reality. We end up saying: *"It will never be different!"* Any seed of renewal is choked before it sees daylight and cynicism wins out. If this were really the case, there would be no amazing stories about human endeavor, no improvement in life, no progress at all. Everything would be frozen into an eternal status quo and, ultimately, stagnation and death.

Change and progress are driven by strong visions and hope and lead to daring enterprises and bold initiatives. Many significant changes originally considered utterly impossible came to be tsunamis of transformation. The Red Cross, for example, emerged from the hopeful vision of a single human being who had witnessed the suffering of those wounded in the Battle of Solferino in 1859. A decade earlier, a physician at a maternity hospital was able to dramatically reduce infections and save countless lives by making doctors and medical students wash their hands and instruments—paving the way for groundbreaking changes in patient care. More recently, modern space technology has enabled us to see detailed photos, taken many millions of miles away, of the surface of Mars, an astounding achievement, given that a century ago—a ridiculously short span of time in our history—space rockets were still a thing of the future.

Our visions and hope make the most improbable things possible. Around the world, we see bold new initiatives emerging out of visions of hope from the realm of creative imagination with its endless potentials and abundance. An audacious and persistent craving for renewal blows through the world like a spring breeze, reminding us to remain true to our inherent nature of innocence and love. Hope becomes the inextinguishable fire of life, a glowing conviction that all good efforts are well spent, regardless of the outcome. Life always finds new ways, and the days of miracles never end. There are navigable pathways ahead where only darkness seems to reign, but even the dark has its own value.

The resolve of hope is focused on wanting the best and following the heart. To do what is truthful and good is not a matter of reward, for it is a reward to know in our essence what we must be and do. Even if we cannot yet perform optimally because we still have things to learn, we do our best and learn from what we do until we improve. In this way, we can partner with the world, remaining faithful to what we find true and beneficial for the greater wholeness we are part of. During the journey, we invite reality to adjust our actions and our course. We are not called to perfection. We are invited to discover the endless unfoldment of the mystery of life. The forgotten land of what-might-be must be rediscovered and reclaimed. It hides like secrets in the deep, green world of the Earth below us, illuminated by the starry heaven above—and we hold the key in our hearts. You and I are the knights of flaming hope, guardians of the impossible possibility, and if we stand as living stones and move as graceful dancers, honoring ourselves and each other in our uniqueness, we can initiate the new journey on the wings of imagination, which will lead us to the promised land of delight and beauty. This is no vague daydream or naïve fantasy. It is the movement of life itself and we are in the company of incredible allies.

⟁ Gift ⟁
Renewal

Give yourself an opportunity to visit the place of renewal. If you wish, this simple exercise can be a way to replenish your energies.

Find a place and time to sit down, relax, and close your eyes. Allow yourself to let go of tensions in your body and enjoy a moment of effortless presence. If you discover any muscle tensions, simply relax and observe yourself witnessing the relaxation. Feel your whole body as a living world full of relaxed energy.

Now focus on your breath and let out a big sigh. Breathe in and then sigh, making whatever sound you want when you breathe out, pausing until it feels natural to breathe in again. If you feel like yawning, do so. Sigh and breathe out, letting it last until the air is out. Then take a third inbreath and let all energy go in the sigh when you breathe out again.

Sense your emotional atmosphere and allow yourself to bathe for a moment in sweetness and soft presence. Enter the emotional state where you can simply enjoy being wrapped in and surrounded by gentleness. Open your heart and let the tender presence permeate through you. Soak it in. Breathe it in. Breathe it out. Gentle sweetness of the tender heart.

Then open your mind to the perceived sensation of rising in light like a bird lifting off the ground. Open your mind to a place of innocence and renewal that really means something to you. It may be any place. Be open and let your longing for a place of wonder and renewal call you. You may already know the place—in which case you can simply go there. If you must first find it within yourself, be completely open and let your longing lead you there. It may be a place you have been to before or an imagined destination—either way, it lives within you and you are visiting it right now.

See the place. What are the sounds there? Is there a special fragrance to it? Does it have a taste? How does it feel? Look around you, right there at the place. What does it give you? Soak in the place. Let it replenish you. Allow yourself to be there as long as it feels right and natural. Don't force anything. Simply allow yourself to be in it and let it fill you up. If inspiration comes, let it come. If you just feel energized, let it come. If you don't experience anything special, but simply appreciate it, let it be as it is.

When you feel it is right, slowly return to your daily activities. The process may take five minutes, ten minutes, or longer, perhaps only three minutes if it comes effortlessly to you. Bring back the renewal and let it out in your life. The renewal itself is like an inbreath and your coming back is the outbreath.

8

THE WINDSINGER

The repetitive, enervating presence of noise
Gradually faded into the background.
Silence emerged like a growing thunder,
Giving way to the world of sounds,
And the precious song,
The roaring song.
The silent song.
The song.

Out of the Noisy Chaos

Everyday life is often a noisy affair. In fact, noise is a way of describing the surface of life when depth is absent. Noise has a chaotic effect. It can bring us out of our center and into an unpleasant drifting where we meander without direction. Surface life or life in flatland is essentially without meaning. It is a homeless survival bereft of the joy and peace that makes us smile. When you are in the noisy world, accepting it as a condition of life, you are part of the noise and echo it through you. You repeat the chatter, the gossip, and the babble, and nothing really makes sense. You are nothing in yourself except a passive spectator, an echo, a bystander in a game that leads to nowhere and makes no sense at all.

And so it is until you start waking up. When does that happen? No one knows but you. When you have had enough, you sign out and leave the scene. This begins when you follow the longing to discover your ground, to find your center, to realize that you are a specific identity, you are a unique presence within a greater presence, and the noisy flatland is like this only when you are fixated on the surface alone. There is depth, there is height, there is wonder and meaning. This is the nature of longing and the awakening from slumber. Hibernation is over, spring is rising. From then on, you gradually start learning to recognize your dance and follow your flow. You partner with life in many ways and learn the language of engagement. It affects you and stimulates your inner dreamer and you start trusting your imagination and follow it to magical places. The path out of the noisy chaos finally takes you to destinations where it is crucial that you find your vocal power and make it heard.

The Sound of You

Sooner or later, you must be able to utter sounds that are truly yours and not just repetitions from other fountainheads. You are the source of your own light, power, and kindness. Don't betray yourself! It will make you into a hollow shadow and you will become wallpaper instead of a distinct room with content. It takes courage—once again—to decide to let your voice be heard. There are many levels of this process, but no steps should be overlooked. Finding your voice is a journey, not a quick fix. In order to discover yourself, you will start mirroring others. This great imitation game is what childhood offers. Remember that childhood has many levels. As an adult, you have matured in some ways, but it is highly likely that you are still like a child in other ways, where you have not yet made yourself heard. Growing up is maturing in so many ways: sexually, mentally, emotionally, practically, individually. When you reach a certain point, there is a leap—or the possibility of a leap—into doing things your own way, or at least attempting to. To make things simple, let me just divide the process of finding your voice into two major steps:

The Outer Call
Your need for success. Your personal visibility. *Your voice.*

The Inner Call
Your deep soul-call. Your essential vocation. *Your song.*

Don't jump over basics. The foundation is that which needs to be the feet, legs, arms, and hands of the further extension or the building and the roof. Finding your personal voice comes first. This means unlocking the qualities you use to step out into visibility and make yourself heard. It is the healthy ego drive to become self-confident in things that really mean something to you. It is no imitation game, but the real sound of you and what you are good at. You need success. You need feedback from the world to let you know that you are recognized for what you do, no matter what it is. This is the outer call, or foundational call. The inner call may come first, but don't ignore the outer part, because that is what generates the power to hold the inner part. What is your sound when you become personally visible? What qualities characterize you as you step forward and make your voice heard?

So, What Is Your Sound?
1 Is it raw and direct—perhaps like rocks, or concrete, or rust, or wooden planks?
2 Is it smooth and effortless—like blank metal, or glass, or perhaps marble?

3 Is it soft and delicate—maybe like silk, or fur, or like a warm carpet?

4 Is it mixed and colorful—like mosaics, or graffiti, or peacock feathers, or a palette?

5 Is it detailed and measured—like letters and numbers, or charts, or schedules?

6 Is it creamy and flowing—like honey, or butter, or maybe like fragrant water?

7 Is it geometric and structured—like ornaments, or configurations, or patterns?

You will probably be able to combine some of the above or think of entirely different "conditions" that go with the sound of you. There may be many more than these seven versions. Play with the ideas and the associations they give you. Mix and match your personal sound with sensory expressions, smells, colors, textures, and tastes. Is your sound urban or nature-based, or a combination of the two? Is your sound like a salsa, hip hop, waltz, or square dance? Sensing and mirroring what you are can be quite a new journey.

Going from here to expressing your sound or voice more clearly than before is another part of the adventure. What you need here is practice and the beginnings may be tough, with many failures and phases of hesitation. Voicing yourself makes you visible. You may occasionally get feedback you don't like, but you must listen and perhaps adjust. Are you too direct? Are you too nice? Are you too smart? Are you too unstable? Are you too rigid? Are you too idealistic? Are you too result-oriented? Where can you learn most? Where does your particular strength lie? In being powerful, kind, bright, graceful, profound, optimistic, effective, or elsewhere? There is much to discover, and it is all about learning the language of voicing yourself. Finding your voice, breathing with your own rhythm and pace, is the prerequisite for starting to sing your song. Give it your time, and if you have opened your voice already, take the time to fully comprehend what its distinguishing feature is, for this is a basic requirement for singing.

The Noble Art of Listening

The inner call brings the essence of you into what you do, to share it with the world. It relies more on self-worth than on self-confidence. It is the being behind the doing, and it brings the deepest need into the equation. Your activities and the type of creativity you display are the outer call. The inner call is your soul-yearning, what makes you deeply joyful and at peace with yourself. The outer call is the body and the inner call is the heart of the body, the animating life pulse. The first is your voice, the second is, as already mentioned, your song. In order to keep track of the quest for your song, you need to learn the noble art of listening.

Being genuinely interested in listening, and not just talking, is essential if you are to learn to express your voice in the world. Listening or attuning is the inhalation and speaking or singing is the exhalation. Together, they become the listening voice and the attuning song. You are the living tuning fork for resonance. Make use of this and be sure to examine other voices as you learn to be your own voice.

LISTENING
Inhalation
Being

SPEAKING
Exhalation
Doing

ATTUNING
Inhalation
Conceiving

SINGING
Exhalation
Creating

When encountering what other people express, and what you express yourself, let it pass through an open-minded, sensitive awareness and explore:

StoneAnchor
Is it deeply grounded?
Does it sound real? Is it grounded in experience? Does it have a ring of truth? Is it kind? Is it genuine? Does it sound clear and distinct?

FlowDancer
Is it in a living flow?
Does it have good timing? Is it open-minded and flexible? Does it sound like a living energy with a healthy vibration? Does it have a specific rhythm?

FireDreamer
Is it creative and inventive?
Does it stimulate my imagination? Does it invite exchange and further development? Does it contain joyful curiosity? Is it playful?

WindSinger
Is it authentic and melodious?
Does it have a kind of musicality? Is it harmonic? Does it carry the vibration of a song in its own way?

When listening to others and to your own voice, keep a sincere interest in how it affects you. Do you feel good in your stomach? Listen to the "inner sounds" in your psyche and be sure to notice when you "taste" something expressed. Examine these angles when listening to others and remember to turn it around—in other words, use exactly the same guidelines when you listen to yourself. This is extremely important. Remember to mirror what you meet and look within yourself with absolute honesty. Don't hide behind facades or clever explanations or any self-image of being nice and kind.

Look with clarity, listen with your whole being. What you learn from your exterior and inherent voices builds the foundation of becoming a singer in your own life and a participant in the greater choir of life.

A Call That Was Heard

Earth Day, April 22, 2017, became a turning point in my life. I heard a song and the foundation of my private world began to crumble. Sussie had thanked me in a mail and sent me a recording of her song to the poem, *The Song of Wandering Aengus,* by W. B. Yeats, and I was changed for good. The way I was earthquaked was much to do with being impacted by a song that roused an undefinable recognition within me. Speech has its advantages and unique qualities and it is a close partner to the mind. Song is different and its qualities reverberate profoundly with the emotional spectrum. My mind was unable to process what was going on, but my feelings and intuition received a message that struck a chord of resonance, a recognition, a remembering of an old *Anam Cara*, a soul friend, who was ultimately to become my colleague, partner, and wife. To me, this was clearly a hearing. I heard a call and I had to answer, by-passing my rational mind and my habitual understanding of who I was.

Hearing is deeply connected with direction. When we hear, physically or within, it comes from a source and a direction. We can dismiss it or respond. To me, responding became a responsibility, a call I could not neglect without betraying my essence, yet it meant that I had to forsake my wife and leave her, something that shook me to the bones. Sometimes, we must do unbelievably hurtful things in order to respond. I must live with the wound and the pain I gave the spouse I loved deeply and continue to love. The note that struck me and the voice I recognized brought incredible pain and indescribable joy, but I had to choose the new path, unable to undo the Gordian Knot in any other way. Following meant leaving. This was described in 'Earthquaked' earlier in Part One of this book.

The new journey was a call that opened to singing. Only weeks after our initial mailing, I sent Sussie some poems by W.B. Yeats, author of *The Song of Wandering Aengus*. Although Sussie had lived in Ireland and received her MA in Traditional Irish Music from the University of Limerick, and created a prizewinning CD with *The Song of Wandering Aengus* as one of the songs on it, she had never heard of George William Russell (AE). I loved his mystical, nature-inspired poems and started sending Sussie selected pieces. She responded immediately with a deep recognition. She felt the poems resonated with a profound part of her, and I started receiving mails and audio files with his poems incorporated into her acappella songs. We both found the very first verse from the AE poem *On a Hillside* evocative and I received her song in less than a month after our first contact:

> "A friendly mountain I know;
> As I lie on the green slope there
> It sets my heart in a glow
> And closes the door on care."

My heart was aglow, so was her's, and in this way, we became muses for each other. AE's delicate and profound nature poems struck a chord that created a shared room for us, and Sussie's voice and melodies seemed to fit like a glove for the Irish verses. Within months, she created more than ten songs, and material for a future release was within reach. Singing became a language that opened a shared space, and within this space, we started making workshops together. These practical working situations also seemed like music as we combined our individual notes into songlines of teaching—two strands of energy interweaving. We recognized each other's keynotes. For Sussie, song is a deep language, and for me, language in its essence is singing. Hearing each other's characteristic tunes was an invitation to create together.

Deep Resonance

It is said that hearing is the first sense we develop and the last sense to leave us. The ear is almost fully developed in the embryo during the fifth month of pregnancy. It is also claimed that dying people continue to listen even after they are no longer able to see, speak, or respond. Gentle speech or song can help them in their transition to other dimensions as they leave the body. Singing to unborn babies makes them respond strongly to specific songs after they have been born.

Do you hear the call of life? What is the message of the call to you? What is your answer? These are not rhetorical questions. They are essentials to a deep and joyful life. Look at this:

Responsible meaning ⟶ *"ability to respond, available"*

Respond meaning ⟶ *"to answer, to pledge"*

Resonate meaning ⟶ *"to sound again, to reverberate"*

We are called, each in our own way, according to our individual nature. We are instruments and sounding boards and are here to vibrate and resonate. This will never succeed if all we do is imitate others. We must listen within in order to notice the vibratory qualities and then take the necessary steps to bring forth our voice and unfold our inner singer. It is not found in other people's expectations of you. It is not found in giving in to social conventions, family traditions, or cultural norms. It may be in harmony with them, but it is not born from outside.

Listening within is a ruthlessly honest exploration, staying true to the core of your nature. From there, it weaves into the pattern of your connections. Certain notes are heard with more clarity than others because we are more attuned to them. Using a sevenfold, energetic spectrum of wholeness, you can ask yourself:

1 Will—Power: Music of Sovereignty

Do I respond and resonate to be in leadership and power and/or to be a spearheading authority for renewal?

2 Feeling—Heart: Music of Gentleness

Do I respond and resonate to be a loving, kind, and empathic presence and/or a wise and understanding companion to others?

3 Thought—Intelligence: Music of Brightness

Do I respond and resonate to be a bright and intelligent thinker and/or a networking source of inspiration?

4 Imagination—Creativity: Music of Wonder

Do I respond and resonate to be an imaginative, creative, transforming agent and/or a beauty-loving artist in my life?

5 Logic—Knowledge: Music of Exploration

Do I respond and resonate to be a resolute, fact-oriented truth-seeker and/or a discoverer of indisputable knowledge?

6 Passion—Faith: Music of Transcendence

Do I respond and resonate to be a devoted idealist and/or an unwavering advocate and activist for the highest good?

7 Action—Results: Music of Manifestation

Do I respond and resonate to be an efficient organizer and/or a result-oriented coordinator and planner?

What music is active in your life? What do you deeply resonate with? Ask yourself: Do I dream of playing this kind of music, or am I already practicing it? You may respond positively to all kinds of music in one way or another but listen closely and with full attention. What is wishful thinking and what is a genuine driving force in you? What awakens you most of all? Selecting three of the seven categories may help you to answer these questions, or you can try to arrange the spectrum in order of priority. Discern where the deepest call is hidden. It is like searching for a hidden treasure. It can be a way of finding your notes in the octave or your colors in the spectrum. Finding your way home is recognizing what makes more sense than anything else. You have all the sounds, but some are more prominent and characterize your essential pattern.

Dare!

Don't get stuck in structures, manuals, and procedures! Never for a moment forget that it is in living that we learn, and not simply in theorizing and observing. There is a huge difference between reading about swimming or cooking and practicing it, or between reading about exotic places and visiting them. Any inspiration from this reading is a suggestion and a call to do things, to step out into the river and feel the water, the temperature, the currents, the driving force, and the flow.

Invite yourself out on a limb and sense what life wants of you, and what you want of life. We are all called to take in the succulent, exquisite nectar of life and transform it into a shining radiance— our gift to the world.

What does it take to become a singer? It takes courage, a delightful longing, and curiosity to open your mouth and be heard. First, you will be heard as a voice, and as you gradually refine it and attune to the notes you sense as yours, it will begin to be heard as a song. Sometimes, when you have a background of experience, it will be sung quickly and with joy. At other times, you will need many years of exercise.

I remember how, more than thirty years back, I worked hard to make each workshop lively and experimental. I had an inner feeling of how it could be, but for many years, I sensed that I never really reached the state I aspired to manifest. People absolutely liked what I did and came back for more. However, I felt dissatisfied as I knew how it could be. These days, I realize that in recent years I have in fact arrived at the place or field I longed for decades ago. Now—luckily—there is a dream of going much further, but I know there is music in what I do. For many years, I was a voice and I voiced out my spirituality as best as I could. Now I accept that I am a singer and part of a greater music, weaving my song lines into a much larger pattern. I have different aspects of my song, professionally, and one of them is as a teacher, another as a coach and SoulFlow guide, and yet another as an author. Besides this, my song must live in my private life as a partner, father, friend, and fellow human being. This part of the daily singing must go naturally hand in hand with the other songs—making a coherent whole.

The language of song has infinite expressions. If you love being a carpenter, a doctor, a baker, a captain, or a caretaker, you have a way of singing in performing those specific activities. What makes it into a song, and not just a voice, is your soul and presence while carrying out your profession. It is your love in doing the things you know very well.

Sometimes, physical singing or dancing can bring a quality into it as well. I remember watching the famous Pike Place Fish Market in Seattle, where employees throw the fish around elegantly and with a smile. I also remember a kind and singing bus driver in Aarhus, the Danish city I was born in. Nor can I ever forget my humming dentist, who, over twenty-five years, completely changed my attitude towards my teeth and taught me how to take good care of them.

Do your singing. Risk it. Dare it. Don't sit back and expect it to occur by itself. Take the daring journey and accept many failures, for you cannot accept not becoming the singer of your life. You will probably irritate and annoy others just by making your voice stronger, simply because you make them aware of their own comfort zone and passive silence. Singing can be very provocative to others, but remember that when you dare to do it, you give others permission to do the same. So, dare it!

◌ GIFT ◌
Song of Freedom, Heart, and Joy

FREEDOM
The song of freedom is an endless call:
"I am always here to be me!"
Raising others when they fall:
"I will help setting them free!"
Its power voice unfetters the flow,
Unleashing the rivers of life.
Celebrating above and below,
To replace all former strife.

Freedom is liberty with no regress,
Truthful to the deepest core,
Expressing to be with a roaring *"Yes!"*
Expanding it more and more.

The freedom song is for you and me,
honoring the oneness of all,
Affirming the grand and majestic *"we!"*
And removing the shady wall.

HEART
The song of the heart is gentle and wild.
Under the sky it can soar,
And rain its presence tender and mild,
Revealing its caring core.

The song of the heart is undyingly kind,
Delicious and full of wonder,
Taking the hand of the open mind,
Awakening humans from blunder.

The heart song supports when there is danger,
Giving the warmth of a gentle embrace,
Never wavering from a stranger,
Simply holding a loving space.
The song of the heart is eternally new.
Its loveliness simply makes sense.
It always falls like refreshing dew
Imbued with the taste of innocence.

JOY

The song of life is the yearning for joy,
As happy children who find
The treasure that no one can ever destroy,
When smiling and laughter align.

The song of joy is the smell of tar,
And the taste of honey from bees.
It is untold stories from near and far
As the whispering, magical breeze.

The lightness of joy is sparkling like stars,
As a hush from a peaceful sleep,
Nature is writing her memoirs,
And no one can gloominess reap.

This is what the world can desire,
And we can affirm in our core:
Let us join the majestic choir,
And cheer on the sunny shore!

9

RIGHT HERE

Most of us do not come to terms with the abysmal truth that *we are what we seek*. It seems to be a hoax. What a disappointment if I should be the goal of the epic adventure of a lifetime! What's special about me? The X-Files hijacked us to believe that "*the truth is out there!*" We have become so blind, deaf, and numb that we search anywhere else but in ourselves. The tragedy is that we tend to sell the real treasure to get fancy bling. Fake news cannot be greater than believing that the treasure is somewhere else out there. It's right here! However, this is not in any way a new story. Goethe's Faust portrays Mephistopheles as the devil's agent, persuading Doctor Faust to make a deal with the devil and pay with his very soul. Selling out is an ancient theme.

We—you and I and all other incredibly valuable human beings—are the living breath reverberating through all existence. Anchoring yourself in your deep identity and connectedness, learning the art of flow in the moment, opening up to the creative imagination, and singing your precious songs are what make this happen and unfold you as the wild breath. In fact, as a soul, your entire life is one long outbreath and the withdrawal from physical life, while returning to the source is your inbreath. The outbreath of the soul is the wave we ride throughout our life, and within this grand movement, we experience lesser waves each year, each day, and each moment. Each birth we witness is intimately related to breathing and how the birthing mother cooperates with the flow of breath. Every ending, ultimately death, is a kind of sigh, a letting go of the withheld air. Breathing in the right way can change all circumstances, in birth, life, and death.

We are used to saying that very special and awesome things or events are breathtaking. Perhaps we should start discovering that life is breathgiving and that you and I are breathgivers when we become singers in the magnificent choir of life.

Rewilding Your Nature

To do this, you must embark on the incredible journey of awakening. This means that you leave the domesticated identity behind you and start "rewilding," a term that comes from nature restoration. Now you need to embrace the inner significance of the same thing. Individual rewilding is your self-conservation, implying that you *"restore and protect your natural processes and core wilderness areas."* You must rediscover your natural wildness, rooted in the fertile and rich earth of your inner depth, gracefully flowing in the fluids and waters of your sensitivity, burning and glowing as the fire of imagination, and blowing as the vibrant wind of your renewing songs. This is the deep, inner climate-change the world needs!

Conscious wildness is the nature of freedom. When you breathe, notice that it is not just in your chest that you inhale and exhale, but deep down in your belly, and it is felt in your whole body, even vibrating out to your fingers and feet. Every part of your organism is vitalized, and your muscles and organs relaxed. Your wildness is your freedom of being present without reservation. Nothing is held back. Not even the jungle mentality of cynical self-protection puts you on guard. You are in relaxed awareness and the world is a miracle. In this condition, you are uncontrollable because you are not tamed and prone to boring repetitions.

What a blessing wildness is! I invite you to open your heart to the fourfold gifts coming from this most wonderful reality:

You as the STONEANCHOR: Deeply grounded $\longrightarrow$ centered, balanced, relaxed, and present

You as the FLOWDANCER: Fluxing in delight $\longrightarrow$ playful, soft and spirited in ever-changing fluidity

You as the FIREDREAMER: Continually imaginative $\longrightarrow$ marveling at new wonders

You as the WINDSINGER: Musically generative $\longrightarrow$ resonating in flowering, living tunefulness

Being alive in this way is a threat to all crystallizing tendencies, all negativity, and all the dull and absent-minded repetitions of things not really enjoyed or understood. You and I need to challenge "business as usual" so that we can start living like never before.

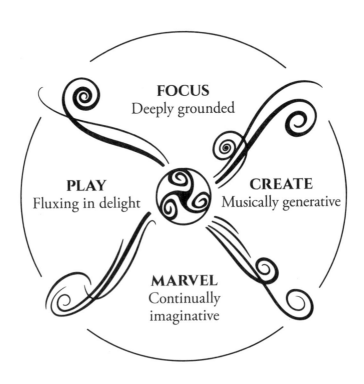

Fragile Abundance

Don't strive for perfection. Give up any silly ideas of being fearless and flawless. You are allowed to fail so that you can learn. You are invited to be fragile and vulnerable. Drop the inclination to live up to certain kinds of images considered more spiritual than others. So many spiritual teachers have been exposed as false and hypocritical as they tried to be leaders above their followers. The fall from so-called heights is not a pretty sight. Nevertheless, it is a great learning exercise in staying natural.

Don't try to live up to things. Be true to where you are. Instead, why not try to be genuine and gentle in your journey towards wildness, and to accept that your position is always a place for great learning? Vulnerability can be a great strength. You are allowed to cry. You are permitted to stumble. You can allow yourself to be exposed because you have nothing to hide. In this way, you become a living example by being you and not by trying to imitate others. It sounds very simple, but many people have great difficulty in practicing it because pressure from others makes it an awkward thing to do. You don't want a photo-shopped version of yourself. You want to reclaim the lost art of being natural. This is the journey of becoming the untamed breath.

It might sound like a self-contradiction that vulnerability and abundance can go hand in hand. However, when you are open in your sensitivity, energy can meet you in new ways. When the living breath becomes your ally, there is access to abundance in new ways. Being vulnerable in this respect means to be trusting, receptive, and confident despite the wounds it could inflict on you. You accept that reality also contains challenges and you decide to stay open. In this way, you invite wonderful things to occur and you are prepared to face headwind as well.

Abundance rests in reciprocity. Life is abundant when you are too. As you open the petals of your life flower, the fragrance from your heart-mind emanate and the world receives the signal that you are accessible.

Inevitably, life around you responds in generous ways and you begin to experience gifts of kindness and support. The natural is full of wonder, and when you partner with life as a fragment of the greater flow, you are invited to receive, delight, and rejoice as you give back in the same spirit. The universe is a living example of continual abundance. From the tiniest particles to the greatest systems, there is an unbroken chain of connectedness and sharing. We are never isolated, no matter how much it may seem so from time to time. We are leaves on the branches of gigantic trees, towering loftily into the Air Sea and rooted in the depth of Mother Earth. Stay fragile so that life can mold you in new ways. Receive the gentle gifts of delight so that you can pass them on in the never-ending chain of renewal and manifestation.

Abundance is sometimes also called synchronicity or meaningful coincidence. When you are ready, life is available with bountiful exchanges. Your vibration attracts similar vibrations and life is multi-dimensional. If the world is usually perceived as a flatland, there is now depth and height as well, and things may occur from these directions. Add to this that the perception of time is usually linear. From a greater perspective, there is instant contact with the past and future too, and not just the dot on the line where you think you are. This is not mumbo jumbo. It is sanity from a larger perspective. Life is full of wonders not because it is irrational, but because it is super-rational. Living in the breath is to respire in a land of plenty instead of gasping in a small, oxygen-deficient room.

Restoring the Villain-Ego

Living in the breath—inviting renewal and being anchored in flow and imaginative song—also means to say goodbye to an old and outworn idea about the so-called ego. Often people have not given a closer thought to what they mean by the ego, but surely it is the supreme villain, the disturber of all peace and tranquility. The ego is the thug, the brute, the moron. Because of this conviction you may hear many different stories about how people try to "*handle the ego.*"

What is the ego? The word *ego* is from Latin and means "I"—the personal consciousness. You could also call it self-conscious awareness. In fact, it is the very foundation for you being "*you*," an identity with certain characteristics. How has this indispensable part of you become the crook, the despised goon of all ages? There may be several answers to this, but it is safe to say that an important part of it is dual, stemming from the concept of the "*sinful person*" in Western Christianity and the "*illusory identity*" in Eastern philosophy, especially Hinduism. I am not opposed to any of these traditions. In fact, they have great depth and value. Nevertheless, a one-sided approach to any tradition quickly leads to severe misunderstandings.

I am sure the shadows hanging over the poor ego, the self-conscious personality, have much to do with these two, religiously motivated views. Being sinful is all about not being good enough, no matter how hard you try. From birth, you are tainted with original sin—the theological notion of mankind's tendency to evil ever since Adam and Eve disobeyed God. You cannot wash it away. All you can do is hope for salvation while you try to forget about yourself and do good to others. The Eastern version has similarities and differences. The essential reality is transcendent and formless. You, living as a manifested form, are not the ultimate truth. Getting yourself out of the equation and stepping back into the source of your essence is the right thing to do. Dissolve your personal identity and you are no more. Getting away from your personal entanglements is to be liberated from the karma wheel of samsara and find release in moksha, ultimate liberation.

Both these views, whether cloaked or pure versions, create a picture of personal identity and ego as something very different from spirituality, which is a great pity, for it is like throwing the baby out with the bathwater. If existence is not a mistake and divinity is the source of all creation, your spiritual identity is the creator of your personal expression. For all its "imperfection," it is a work in progress and a gradual awakening on the journey of unfoldment. At your core, you are a spiritual being and it is in your nature to express yourself.

As part of the creative universe, you exercise being a creator in your own way. A crucial part of this is developing an instrument that can be used to play your music and sing your songs. This instrument is your self-consciousness and its breathing, organic form, where the "I," or ego, is the focus for learning and maturing. The ego is your dear friend on the journey of awakening. Don't treat it like trash! It is the dear, personal you, striving, struggling to get a foothold in the stream of life.

The unfoldment of your nature requires that your ego or personal identity be treated the same way you treat others. You, the greater identity, can embrace your personality and restore it, back from its enforced role as the ultimate villain. If you do that, you express the appreciating tenderness that is needed, and you help the maturing personality to take part in your being of light, love, and power. In this way, you help it to breathe naturally, find its voice, and discover its deeper sound—and you ultimately teach it to sing. Be gentle and befriend your maligned and excluded ego. You will be amazingly rewarded by this compassionate and wise act.

Pause

It is in the pausing that everything happens. Experiencing your breath is a way to discover this. The pausing between inhalation and exhalation may seem like an abyss between two flowing movements, but it can also be experienced as an opening to infinity. I say "pause" because something does indeed come to an end or cease. We rarely live in this in-between, perhaps because we regard it as being connected to death. Most people fear death. The very idea of cessation is petrifying to many. Living on the surface of constant activity, not breathing but panting, is an escape from depth and height. *"Life is what happens to you while you're busy making other plans"*—these words by Allen Saunders, later popularized by John Lennon in his song *"Beautiful Boy,"* are spot on. Fleeing from the here and now is extremely costly as we use so much energy to keep reality away. It becomes an attachment to sentimental aspects of the past and an anticipation that the future will bring something good. The only thing we desert is the present.

Pausing is a coming back to the focus. It is like pressing your head through a low ceiling and breathing in the fresh air under the vast sky. Sometimes, the quietness is one of the surprises you may experience. Suddenly, you are in a place of gigantic proportions and there is silence. You may begin to hear sounds reverberating in the vastness of this enormous space. Pause and listen. This is the greater life.

Pausing is the wonder of *in-betweenness*. The vastness of the *after-then and not-yet*. The miracle of the now is that it is never the same. There is always a possibility of renewal and refreshment if you open yourself to it. Just pause. Just sense the moment. If you do this often, you will be able to experience how you learn to navigate the in-between. It is a new realm opening to undreamed-of possibilities. Think for a moment about any significant pause you have had in your life. Was it perhaps something like this?

On holiday, you are stunned by a view.

It is raining, and your eyes catch sight of a drop running down a window.

During a concert, the singer stops, and everything is quiet before the final tune.

For a second, you can hear the drop of a needle in a room full of people.

Alone with yourself, you suddenly realize that nobody is there, only you. You turn off the smartphone and give in to the sensation of being in your body.

Smelling a flower, you forget everything else and there is just the fragrance.

Looking into the eyes of another person, time stops.

Pauses are the windows to eternity and infinity. Befriending these rare guests may bring deep magic into the breath of your life and make them return more frequently. A sense of refreshing greatness comes into the moment, wherever you happen to be. This is a possibility to discover that the quality of silence can permeate any moment full of chatter and noise. Depth can saturate any flatness and bring it a new aliveness. It is a coming back. You step out of a small room and respire in a grand space, where you reconnect with a greater meaning of life.

Return to your breath whenever you are stressful. Reconnecting with your breath is a continued coming home. Just be aware and return. Breathing is where you are.

∽ GIFT ∾
Wind-Shower

Give yourself the gift of connecting with the wind in much the same intimate way that you connect with water when you take a shower. It is a beneficial and ultra-simple practice.

It may be the gentle breeze in the trees, making its distinct sounds in the leaves or pine needles. It may be an open space with a view accessible to you. It may be in the backyard of your garden, if you have one, or in a nearby park. Make it enjoyable to find a place—or more places—if you prefer.

Find your place and take a little time to settle down so that you are comfortable. You can stand or sit, even lie down. You can do the exercise while walking, but it is a very good, grounding experience to start when your body is quietly at rest.

Relax your body. Sense where you are. Use a minute or so to orient yourself and feel your position in the surroundings—cityscape or landscape. Notice what is around you.

Then listen to the wind and feel it touching your skin, how it touches your clothing and your hair. Tune in to the wind. Sense how it is everywhere and affects everything. Listen to the sounds it creates.

Listen to the tunes of the wind. Observe how leaves or other things are moved by the wind, and how you are moved by it. Attune to the wind. Greet the wind. Befriend the wind.

Then feel your breath. Your breathing is your internal wind. Feel how your inner wind breathes through your body as you are surrounded by the outer wind. Feel how the inner and outer winds are related as ebb and flow, as changing waves.

Then shower in the outer and inner wind. They are the same. You are permeated with your inner wind and caressed by the outer wind. Become the wind. Become the breath. Wind is all there is, everywhere. The breath is pulsating within and around you, and you let go of all tensions, all restraints. You *are* the wind; you *are* the shower.

Do this as long as it feels natural. Then slowly return to your normal activities, bringing the magical touch of the living wind back with you. Wind-showers are a blessing—be blessed so that you can pass on the spirit of the wind.

Deeply Connected

There is a profound beauty in the noble art of breathing. You never breathe alone. We are always connected through breath. We often forget that we are connected by more than just by our verbal communication, actions and social exchange, by body language and gestures, or by smartphones and the Internet. There is a radically simple way of being together that we often overlook or ignore. This ultrasimple way of connecting is just to be silent and breathe together. Through socialization, we are taught to talk, to exchange viewpoints and experiences using words, and our body language follows this preferred way of exchanging. The mere thought of being silent when other people are present can be quite scary, especially if we do not know each other well.

However, it can be liberating to remain silent and breathe together—something many people are unfamiliar with as it can be quite an intimate experience. If you are fortunate enough to be able to meditate with others, you may already have shared wonderful times where the only sound you hear is the breathing. Being close to dying people can also be revealing as there comes a moment when verbal communication fades into the background, and the preferred togetherness is a warm and heartful silence. In such a situation, breathing together can be a spontaneous discovery. Another way to experience the beauty and depth of the living breath is to sleep in the presence of another person or to gently hold a sleeping baby. The deep reality beyond words can become a treasure full of wonders.

Even speech can become a gateway to the breath if you can experience the beauty of a person speaking with a graceful connection to the breath. Being together, speaking in a peaceful way in which the breath becomes part of the presence, and where moments of silence can complement the words, truly is a rewarding and renewing experience. Given the present circumstances, where noise plays a huge role every day, and where continued activity fills out the rare gaps of quietness, it is quite a thing to explore the wisdom and beauty of the shared breath and the fellowship of silence. As you increasingly release yourself into the world of the untamed breath, you will find opportunities to make space for shared breath and renewing silence. Don't delay what you can start already. Make space for deep connectedness and give others the gift of cherishing it. Many will seize the opportunity if invited to do so.

You Untamed—Inspire!

Letting yourself loose in the world is the long-awaited blessing! Don't hold yourself back and betray yourself and the universe. Follow the flow of your urge to sing. It comes from your ElvenHeart as it unfolds and merges with your Human Heart and they become one.

When you express your nature in creative acts, in your daily life and activities, you engage with inspiration. Not surprisingly, the word inspiration comes from the Latin *inspirare*, which actually means "*breathing in spirit.*" When you follow the call of your wild heart, you unleash your Pegasus and soar. You allow yourself to be uplifted and filled with the wonderful ideas and spontaneous impulses that can bring new life to you and others. It is a delightful inhalation that will ultimately be exhaled in visible, tangible changes.

You are a breathgiver because you are a breathtaker. You partake in the great reciprocity, the ever-changing rhythm of life. Who can say what will inspire you? Nobody except you. You hold the secret key to unlock the gifts of your being. No guru can deposit it. No authority can claim it. No power can take it from you, as it can flower only through you. You are the guru. You are the authority. You are the power.

Standing in your Land you are deeply anchored in your bedrock. From here arises a silent power—your sovereignty, your birthright to be a portal between worlds, and your dignity because of what you are, a unique identity in the greatness of life.
STONEANCHOR—Stand in your full connectedness!

Deeply embedded in the fruitful world of life, you follow the dancing movements of the water and become the dancer in your life. In the midst of abundance, you whirl in celebration of life and in oneness with your co-dancers. You are the one that displays the wonder of life.
FLOWDANCER—Dance the world into being!

Merged with the sacred space from where the healing fountains derive, and where the great waters mirror the mature gentleness from the flushing evening sun, you are wrapped in the deep, smiling peace. You are always a creative thread in the tapestry of life, interwoven with all other strands.
FIREDREAMER—Weave the mantle of peace!

Connected with the greenness of the grass and the morning wind, blowing through the undisturbed landscapes, you connect with the sweeping breeze that brings eternal change and living flow. You are a friend of the wind and the youthful dawn.
WINDSINGER—Proclaim the life of renewal!

Afterglow

Let's imagine. Let's step into the in-between. Let's stay for a magical moment in the betwixt and between, neither in the past, present or future.

What may emerge when you and I and our Sidhe partners step into our **StoneAnchor** reality, our *Stone of Destiny*, take authority in our deep connectedness, and learn the art of merging the Sidhe-connections and resources with creating the Human-manifestations and results?

Fluid Connectivity $\longrightarrow$ $\longleftarrow$ **Fixed Manifestation**

What may emerge when you and I and our Sidhe partners step into our **FlowDancer** reality, our *Cauldron of Plenty*, start sharing abundance and reciprocity, and learn the art of merging the Sidhe-Starry Brilliance of the Illumined Heart with the Human-Fiery Glow of the Compassionate Heart?

Bright Starlight $\longrightarrow$ $\longleftarrow$ **Warm Compassion**

What may emerge when you and I and our Sidhe partners step into the **FireDreamer** reality, our *Spear of Victory*, making the wonders of renewal unfold, and learn the art of merging the Sidhe-imagination and lyrical joy with the Human-reasoning and logical reliability?

Lyrical Imagination $\longrightarrow$ $\longleftarrow$ **Logical Reason**

What may emerge when you and I and our Sidhe partners step into the **WindSinger** reality, our *Sword of Light*, bringing lifegiving sound into the world, and learn the art of merging the Sidhe-plasticity and singing flow with the Human-persistency and one-pointed, purposeful voice?

Plasticity $\longrightarrow$ $\longleftarrow$ Persistency

Celebrating our Star-Gaian Sidhe-Humanity
In service of All Life
Might be Full of Wonders

The Four Sacred Hallows
Might come together again
In you and me and in our Sidhe co-creators

The Magic might be released again
Into the world

The HumanHearts in their Sidheness
Might blossom

The ElvenHeart in our Humaneness
Might blossom

The wind swept over mountains and hills
With a breath of life and a whisper of joy
Great Mother Earth was teeming with thrills
The streams and rivers were young and coy
And I saw the world through the eyes of a Sidhe
And I gazed at the promise of dawn
How shall this be?

The world unfolded its youth and mirth
Forth came dare together with pride
Innocence forgotten in death and birth
And it gradually led to the great divide
And I saw the world through the eyes of a Sidhe
And I wept over pain and farewells
How can this be?

Ages unfolded and tales were told
Of human ways in blindness and vain
Amidst the highlands and valleys of soul
There was learning together with gain
And I saw the world through the eyes of a Sidhe
And I whispered: Is there another way?
How may this be?

Chaos emerged with destruction and war
Earth was in peril and Paradise lost
Yet, something was stirring in the human core
Would it be in time, and how about the cost?
And I saw the world through the eyes of a Sidhe
And I laughed as I glimpsed a pathway ahead
How might this be?

From the wild came a song completely untamed
Something was moving in the human heart:
"Awake for reunion—wholeness reclaimed!"
Sidhe and humans learning the art
And I saw the world through the eyes of a Sidhe
And I smiled beholding a new world emerge
How will this be?

ILLUSTRATION CREDITS

p 40 John Duncan: The Riders of the Sidhe, 1911—Public Domain, Wikipedia

p 44 William Butler Yeats—Public Domain, Wikipedia

p 44 George William Russell—Public Domain, Wikipedia

p 47 Søren Hauge: Symbol of Human Kingdom—elements from Shutterstock

p 49 Søren Hauge: Symbol of Deva Kingdom—elements from Shutterstock

p 51 Søren Hauge: Symbol of Sidhe Kingdom—elements from Shutterstock

p 65 Jeremy Berg: The Howe from the Card Deck of the Sidhe

p 65 Entrance to Bryn Celli Ddu, Anglesey—Public Domain, Wikipedia

p 74 Søren Hauge (photo): Poskær Stenhus—Stone Barrow at Mols Bjerge in Jutland, Denmark

p 83 Ron Hays (photo): Sidhe-portal with the Sidhe Glyph at its center

p 86 Søren Hauge (photo): Ben Bulben, County Sligo, Ireland

p 93 Søren Hauge (photo): Deborah Koff-Chapin making Touch Drawing of Sidhe at Findhorn

p 93 Deborah Koff-Chapin: Touch Drawing of Sidhe at Findhorn

p 113 Jakob Hauge Reitz: Triskelion

p 120 Søren Hauge: The Four Hallows—elements from Shutterstock and Internet

p 138   Søren Hauge: The Four Portals—elements from Shutter-
         stock and Internet
p 141   Søren Hauge: StoneAnchor—elements from Shutterstock
         and Internet
p 155   Søren Hauge: FlowDancer—elements from Shutterstock
         and Internet
p 158   Søren Hauge: Playhouse and Breath
p 168   Søren Hauge: FireDreamer—elements from Shutterstock
         and Internet
p 184   Søren Hauge: WindSinger—elements from Shutterstock
         and Internet
p 188   Tuning Forks: Shutterstock
p 200   Søren Hauge: Focus—Play—Marvel—Create—elements
         from Shutterstock

Selected Literature and Websites

Berg, Jeremy. *Faerie Blood*. Traverse City, MI: Lorian Press, 2013.

———. *A Knight to Remember—Visions with the Sidhe*. Traverse City, MI: Lorian Press, 2015.

Blamires, Steve. *The Cronicles of the Sidhe*. Cheltenham, Gloucestershire: Skylight Press, 2012.

Evans-Wentz, W. Y. *The Fairy Faith in Celtic Countries*. Mineola, NY: Dover Publications, Inc., 2002.

Froud, Brian and John Matthews. *How to See Faeries*. New York: Abrams, 2011.

Gelder, Dora van. *The Real World of Fairies: A First-Person Account*. Wheaton, IL: Quest Books, 1999.

Hauge, Søren. *The Wild Alliance*. Traverse City, MI: Lorian Press, 2015.

Hodson, Geoffrey. *The Kingdom of Faerie*. Adya, Chennai: The Theosophical Publishing House, 1927.

Matthews, John. *The Moon Oracle of the Sidhe*. Traverse City, MI: Lorian Press, 2017.

———. *The Sidhe: Wisdom from the Celtic Underworld*. Traverse City, MI: Lorian Press, 2004.

———. *The Sidhe Oracle of the Fleeting Hare*. Traverse City, MI: Lorian Press, 2018.

———. *Walking with the Sidhe—Oracles and Visions from the Celtic Otherworld*. Traverse City, MI: Lorian Press, 2019.

Pogačnik, Marko. *Universe of the Human Body*. Great Barrington, MA: Lindisfarne Books, 2016.

Russell, George William (AE). *The Candle of Vision*. Ithaca, NY: Cornell University Library, 2009.

———. *Collected Poems*. Rockville, MD: Wildside Press, 2008.

———. *The Descent of the Gods: The Mystical Writings of G. W. Russell—A.E.* Edited and introduced by Raghavan and Nandini Iyer. Gerrards Cross, UK: Colin Smythe Ltd., 1988.

Spangler, David. *Conversations with the Sidhe*. Traverse City, MI: Lorian Press, 2014.

———. *Engaging with the Sidhe*. Traverse City, MI: Lorian Press, 2017.

———. *Subtle Worlds: An Explorer's Field Notes*. Traverse City, MI: Lorian Press, 2010.

———. *Working with Subtle Energies*. Traverse City MI: Lorian Press, 2016.

Spangler, David and Jeremy Berg. *Manual to Card Deck of the Sidhe*. Traverse City, MI: Lorian Press, 2011.

Stewart, R. J. *Earth Light*. Rockville, MD: Mercury Publishing USA, 1998.

———. *Power Within the Land*. Rockville, MD: Mercury Publishing USA, 1998.

———. *The Living World of Faery*. Rockville, MD: Mercury Publishing USA, 1999.

———. *The Well of Light: From Faery Healing to Earth Healing*. Arcata, CA: R.J. Stewart Books, 2004.

Yeats, W. B. *Collected Poems*. Macmillan Collector's Library. London: Macmillan, 2016.

Yeats, W. B. (Comp.) *The Book of Fairy and Folk Tales of Ireland*. Vacaville, CA: Bounty Books, 2016.

Selected Websites

Lorian Association: www.lorian.org
Lorian Press (Jeremy Berg): www.lorianpress.com
Portals Connect: www.portalsconnect.com
Elven Gates (Ron Hays): www.elvengates.com
Touch Drawing (Deborah Koff-Chapin): www.touchdrawing.com
Søren Hauge: www.sorenhauge.com/english

GRATITUDE

I am deeply grateful to many, many people who have made this book possible, and who have contributed to it in one way or another. First, I need to thank my friend and colleague, David Spangler, who has been indispensable in the whole process. I simply don't know where I would be, had he not been the crucial catalyzer for helping me to trust my own process. Besides this, his books and teaching about the Sidhe constitute the deepest inspiration I have received in this whole field. Secondly, I want to thank my other friend and colleague, Jeremy Berg, who has been an amazing source of inspiration and support. Besides David and Jeremy, all my friends in the Lorian Association—named and unnamed—are an incredibly talented group of people and peers, and their approach to the Sidhe have been and continue to be a great source of upliftment and insight, and I realize through all these trusted people how much is in the making in the Sidhe field these years. Special thanks to Ron Hays, Deborah Koff-Chapin, Rue Hass, Timothy Hass, Vance Martin, Lucinda Herring, Freya Secrest and Julia Spangler for inspiration and support.

The same goes for the awesome people at Findhorn who have taken the Sidhe flame into their own lives and manifested it in their ways. Special thanks to Thomas Miller, Mary Inglis, Carolina Bonifacino, Sohini Sinha and all the responsible people for the Co-Creative Spirituality Conference at Findhorn in 2018 where the Sidhe were presented in a larger scale for the first time, and the Sidhe event

Sussie and I held there in October 2019. Thank you from my heart to Sabine Weeke from Findhorn Press who reached out to me regarding this book. Also great thanks to Ruth Richmond, Michael Skeeter and his network who invited me as teacher to Fairy Congress at Skalitude Retreat. Also, warm thanks to Michael Lindfield, Board President of Meditation Mount in Ojai, California, for warm support in my Sidhe endeavor.

The warmest thanks to all participants on my more than 30 Sidhe-workshops and Sidhe-group Journeys in Denmark, Norway, England, The Faroe Islands, Ireland and US. It is not possible for me to express the wealth of creativity and co-sharing this has created, and the unexpected blessings it has given, as well as ideas for further growth and activity. All the wonderful contributors in this book are a great testimony of how the whole Sidhe-field is unfolding. Thank you to all of you, Jes Romme, Alice Weibull, Annegrete Bugtrup, Eva Søborg Larsen, Christel Schneidermann, Annette Pomiklo, Sheena Mariah Nielsen, Elisabeth Dyrmose, Joan Kragh, Belinda Bell, Jane Folsted, Carolina Nuti, Ron Hays, Deborah Koff-Chapin and Jeremy Berg.

Huge thanks to my very special and trusted friend and colleague, Kenneth Sørensen, for unwavering support regarding my endeavors in this relatively new territory. To my life-partner and colleague, Sussie Luscinia Nielsen, I owe uncountable things for all the inspiration and sharing we experience in this field that brought us together, and has led us to workshops, journeys and the Sidhe-songs you unfold with such grace and beauty.

Gratitude to you!

ABOUT THE AUTHOR

Photo by Sussie Luscinia Nielsen

Søren Hauge (born 1961) is a Danish spiritual teacher, counselor, and author. For three decades, he was a leader, teacher, and organizer within the holistic groups and associations in Scandinavia. He has an MA in the history of ideas and philosophy from Aarhus University and many years of experience working with interreligious dialogue. Together with Kenneth Sørensen, he is co-developer of a new Energy Typology and the SoulFlow Method, a psychospiritual healing approach. Since 2007, he has worked with David Spangler and the Lorian Association. Søren organizes spiritual group journeys in different countries, facilitates workshops, gives lectures, and has a private practice as a spiritual counselor. He is father to two adult daughters and lives with his wife, Sussie Luscinia, and her daughter in central Zealand, Denmark.

For more information, visit: **www.sorenhauge.com**

By the Same Author in English

The Wild Alliance—Lorian Press, 2015
Untamed Breath—Forlaget WiseHeart, 2019

By the Same Author in Danish

Rosenkreuzerne (The Rosicrucians)—Sankt Ansgars Publishers, 1990

Det skjulte Menneske (Hidden Man) —Borgens Publishers, 1996

Selvopdagelsens Kunst (The Art of Self-Discovery)—Borgens Publishers, 1999

Landskabstempler (Landscape Temples)—Visdom Publishers, 2000

Daggry for Verden (Planetary Dawn)—Levende Visdom Publishing, 2004

Teosofiens Verden (The World of Theosophy)—Levende Visdom Publishing, 2006

Levende Visdom (Living Wisdom)—Lemuel Books, 2008

Barack Obama (with Asger Lorentsen)—Lemuel Books & Gyldendal, 2009

Shakespeare Mysteriet (The Shakespeare Mystery)—Lemuel Books, 2010

Dine Syv Holotyper (with Kenneth Sørensen) (Your Seven Holotypes)—Kentaur Publishers, 2010

Ildens Rejse (Journey of Fire)—WiseHeart Publishing, 2012

Englen i dig (The Angel within You)—Lemuel Books, 2012

Sidhe—Elverkraften (Sidhe—The Elvenforce)—Lemuel Books, 2014

Vild Spiritualitet (Wild Spirituality)—WiseHeart Publishing, 2014

Det Glemte Land (The Forgotten Land)—WiseHeart Publishing, 2016

SoulFlow—frisæt dit liv (SoulFlow—Set your Life Free)— WiseHeart Publishing, 2016

Elefantsprog (Elephant Language)—WiseHeart Publishing, 2017

Also of Interest from Findhorn Press

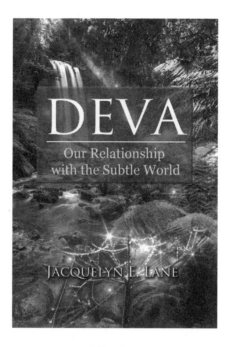

Deva
by Jacquelyn E. Lane

As the world's form builders, the symphony at the heart of Creation, the energy of Deva is intrinsic to all that we experience. Jacquelyn E. Lane explores how we can partner with Deva in our everyday lives to evolve both our kingdom and theirs. Introducing the hierarchy of the Deva kingdom, from elementals and nature spirits to higher Deva and the levels in between, she examines the metaphysics that underlie their existence and offers a glimpse of their wisdom, humor, and joy. A tapestry of the author's experiences with the intelligence that is the Deva kingdom, *Deva* is a workable, integrated philosophy of how we can evolve into a higher human destiny. It is a call to all who care about life on "our" planetary home and an invitation to a deeper understanding, relationship and cooperation with that life.

ISBN 978–1–64411–074–4